"My Mama Wrote It!"

12/18/10

To Patty

God Bless

Pat Harris-Look

"My Mama Wrote It!"

Writings and Compilations of My Mother,
Mrs. Louisteen Bolding-Harris

Patricia L. Harris-Cook, Daughter

Copyright © 2008 by Patricia L. Harris-Cook, Daughter.

Library of Congress Control Number: 2008907363
ISBN: Softcover   978-1-4363-6414-0

All rights reserved. No part of this book may be reproduced or transmitted in any form or by any means, electronic or mechanical, including photocopying, recording, or by any information storage and retrieval system, without permission in writing from the copyright owner.

This book was printed in the United States of America.

To order additional copies of this book, contact:
Xlibris Corporation
1-888-795-4274
www.Xlibris.com
Orders@Xlibris.com
52623

Contents

Introduction 9

Chapter 1   Welcome Addresses 11

Chapter 2   Responses..15
                     "Honored One"..19

Chapter 3   Resolution 20
                     Tribute To An Usher..20
                     Obituaries 24
                     Rules and By-Laws 25

Chapter 4   Words of Wisdom 27

Chapter 5   Great Scriptures References..30
                 Scriptures that make you say "WOW!"

Chapter 6   Speeches for All Occasions 40
                     "The Importance of a Beautiful Tongue"......................40
                     "Education—A Privilege"..44
                     "A Pattern of Thinking—The 23rd Psalms"................45

Chapter 7   Readings...49
                     "The Lord's Prayer"...49
                     "The Influence of a Christian Woman in the
                         Church"..54
                     "How Women Can Win Souls To Christ"....................56
                     "Women of the Bible" 58
                         -Trivia-...61

Chapter 8   Essay: "The American Home—Our Greatest Heritage" 64
                     Stories—Philosophies—Hope Thoughts—Insights....65

Chapter 9   Term Papers 81

Chapter 10   Play: "The Travelers Guide to Heaven" 107

Chapter 11   Biography of "My Mama" 114

                 Mama's Favorite Recipes 120

**SPEECHES, ADDRESSES, AND READINGS
FOR VARIOUS OCCASIONS:**

Writings by: My Mama; Mrs. Louisteen Bolding-Harris

Author: Patricia L. Harris-Cook

Introduction

—"My Mama Wrote it!"

My Mama's unique gift in writing talents, and skills offers many opportunities to put her words and writing to use in witnessing and spreading God's word.

Audiences that this book is preferably written for, or the purpose in putting this book together is for Christian women, and women in Mission Unions (WMUs), especially in the Baptist Church. Any other church person interested or needing ideas in writing and critiquing speeches for church presentations will enjoy also.

The book will aid biblical scholars needing quick references in finding background scriptures for bible study and lessons, which these writing will help.

Some of Mama's papers were lost, but the ones found were written from her records and journals. Basically each item was recorded to help the reader, and enlighten those in doubt or who cannot find in the bible what they are looking for. There are no set doctrines, each person can find information that suits him or her as needed. My Mama read and interpreted the Bible for herself and wrote accordingly.

This book, "My Mama Wrote It," offers you, the reader the opportunities to share in Mama's writings, study God's word, and a service to others in need of quick talks already prepared in welcoming people to church festivities, responding to welcomes presented, and whatever talk needed in a moments notice. Included in the book are obituaries and resolutions, which will help in limited time schedules after death, etc.

Each church, no matter what denomination can find excerpts which can be used, or that will uplift you in times of need, fear, or depression. Mama's term papers, essays, play, and speeches, are to help youth and adults in their writing skills and presentation. My Mama loved writing, this is why I write this book in dedication to her great talent.

May God bless each reader. Thank You

Patricia L. Harris-Cook, Author/Daughter

Chapter 1

Welcome Addresses

Written by: My Mama

WELCOME: [For Women's Meetings]

Dear Sisters in Christ we welcome you tonight to this precious sisterhood in Christ Jesus. We want you to realize how grateful we are to you and others like you who serve so fervently in the missionary interests of our Lord's Kingdom from day to day.

You ladies have shown us that the highest purpose of your lives is to share the love of Christ Jesus with all people. "Ye are the light of the world," said Christ. We welcome you because you are light to a dark world. "Neither do men light a candle, and put it under a bushel, but on a candlestick, and it giveth light unto all that are in the house." "Let your light so shine among men that they may see your good works and glorify your Father which is in heaven." Because we feel that you are sincerely striving to shine through good missionary works, not for your own glory but for the glory of God, we welcome you. You are ever welcome here because you serve the Lord, and may He ever bless you and through you, bless others, is our prayer for you.

WELCOME:
With the Psalmist we can say this evening, "I was glad when they said let us go into the house of the Lord." We are glad to be in His House, and doubly glad tonight because we are in company with such sincere and enthusiastic Christians. We are glad that you have come to share this program with us today. You have bestowed upon us a great honor just by merely being here with us.

We know that you are always at home when you enter the house of the Lord, but be assured that in this house you are more welcome than ever. Our organization is looking forward to the inspiration you have planned to bring us and I am sure much good will come from our meeting together here today.

There are so many opportunities given us day after day and today we feel that the Lord has sent you to us for a very special purpose—the opportunity to engage in worthwhile work for His sake and for his glory.

Welcome to our Church and may God bless every word spoken, every contact made and every thought which has gone into the preparation of this wonderful occasion.

WELCOME:
We of the _____ appreciate the interest you have shown by coming to our program this evening. We bid you welcome and hope that you will feel so at home that you often come back to see us on other occasions. It is a pleasure to welcome our friends for it is our friends who bring us our greatest happiness in this world of passing values.

Words fail to flow as I try to tell you how blessed we consider ourselves to have you present, but I hope before the evening is gone you will feel as happy and delighted to be here with us as we are to have you.

WELCOME:
This is indeed an honor dear friends in Christ, to have you in our midst. We appreciate you taking time out from your many activities to join with us this evening. We know that you are busy doing many worthwhile tasks for our Lord, but God can always count on folks who are already busy, to be about their Father's business at all times. Just your being here has shown to

us that you have the same feeling for the Lord's House and the Lord's work as we do. We want to make you comfortable and entertain you so that you can say, "It has been good for us to be here, I'm glad I came . . ." Welcome to _____, Welcome, Welcome, Welcome!

WELCOME:

In reverence to Almighty God, Pastor _____, Pulpit guest, the M.C., Christians and friends: I am elated to bring you words of Welcome here today. We feel highly honored to share this occasion with you. We thank our dear Heavenly Father for this beautiful Day and we know that we are going to have a joyous time as we fellowship together.

Feel free to sing, pray, shout . . . anything that you do at your church, please feel free to do the same here. As I stand here and gaze upon you in your beautiful white dresses, etc., a splendid picture comes to mind. I am made to think of a Heavenly Scene where Angels are waiting upon our Lord.

Dear Missionaries you are like angels as the deeds you perform are angelic—continue the great work you are doing, and when it is yours to quit or cease this way of life, you will hear words of Welcome coming from Him, who is by far more worthy than anyone who ever lived, say "YOU ARE WELCOME." Thank You!

WELCOME:

Giving honor to God, Pulpit, Guests, Our Pastor _____, Mistress of Ceremony and Christian Friend. It is an honor for me to stand before you this evening to extend this warm Welcome. We want you to know that it comes from (Church), and (Pastor). You are welcome to worship with us at all times. Thank You.

WELCOME:

Giving honor to God, Pastor, Pulpit, Guest, Visitors and Friends. I am elated to bring you words of welcome. We feel highly honored to share this occasion with you.

We thank our dear heavenly Father for sending His Son as a tiny little baby, into the world to pay for all our sins. As we welcome everyone here today, Let us praise the Lord for His wonderful gift to all mankind.

(Silent Prayer—All heads bowed for one minute) Amen.

Let us continually praise and thank God for his wonderful gift to all mankind. Thank you Lord for all your gifts, prayers and encouragement.
(Bow heads and say), "Thank You!

WELCOME:

In Reverence to the Almighty God, Pastor, Pulpit guest, the Mistress of Ceremony, Christians and Friends. Dear Sisters in Christ, we welcome you today to this sisterhood in Christ Jesus

We want you to know how grateful we are to you for your attendance and presence today. You ladies have shown us that the highest purpose of your lives is to share the love of Christ Jesus with all people. "Ye are the light of the world." said Christ. We welcome you because you are light to a dark world."

"Neither do men light a candle, and put it under a bushel but on a candlestick and it giveth light unto all that are in the house."

"Let your light so shine among men that they may see your good works and glorify your Father which is in Heaven." Because we feel that you are sincerely striving to shine through good missionary works, not for your own glory, but for the glory of God, We Welcome You. You are ever welcome here because you serve the Lord and may He ever bless you and through you bless others is our prayer for you.

Chapter 2

Responses *(To Welcome Addresses)*

RESPONSE:
To The Pastor, Mistress of Ceremony, Chairperson of Woman's Day Activities, Friends and Co-Workers.

We thank you for your very gracious welcome on this wonderful occasion of your Woman's Day Service.

We are grateful for your hospitality, and kindness to us in inviting us to share this great day of the year with you.

Our earnest prayer is that we may always keep Christ first in all our plans, as you have done today, and that we may ever work together as women who seek to bring lost souls into the kingdom of Christ here on earth.

RESPONSE:
The fellowship we feel here within these hallowed walls is good for us; we feel drawn very close to your great organization and are happy to be among your group. I feel that words are inadequate when I try to express my gratitude to you for your cordial welcome. But, may I say in my feeble way, "Thank You," for including us on your great program and in your lists of guest.

RESPONSE: Friends and Associates:
On behalf of the guests here assembled, I receive and accept your beautiful words of welcome with much pleasure, first, because of the happy spirit in which it was extended; second, because it comes to us as an expression of love and appreciation for our presence here.

I assure you, we will treasure your choice words of welcome, long feel the warmth of the hospitality and fellowship so impressively made in your fine welcome.

Already, since being in your presence, we have been inspired—our minds have been given much food for thought, and the very fine way you have carried this great affair, be-speaks the sincerity of the magnanimous spirit that fills your hearts.

My earnest hope is that you will continue in this good way of giving encouragement and inspiration to the people. I congratulate you, and bid you God-speed in the successful accomplishment of the glorious task set before you. You are yet in the ascendancy of your meridian height, continue to press your claim, with self-determination naught but death can stop, and more glorious success will reward you ere the day is done.

I thank you for the honor given me, in responding to the address of welcome, and for your patience and most friendly reception.

As you were speaking, we felt that you must be psychic, for you have said just the words which makes us feel welcome indeed, and we do appreciate warmth and cordiality. Our hearts are filled to overflowing and we feel the presence of our Lord here tonight in this wonderful gathering. Our sincere hope is that we may bring some inspiration that will draw you even closer to our Lord and Savior Jesus Christ.

RESPONSE:
Mistress of Ceremony, Pastor, Visiting Friends and All Our Charming Host and Hostesses:

We have a feeling tonight that we are indeed among Christian friends and we are sure of our welcome. We felt that we were invited because you wanted us to share with you your good fortune. I am sure each of us will be greatly benefited by our presence here tonight and we are assured that God must be pleased as He looks down upon His children and sees the fine spirit in which they are sharing the blessings of His work.

We all know our duties and responsibilities as Christian men and women, but so often we have to be reminded that we are not quite fulfilling them to the best of our ability, and God does require of us that we do our best. God is so good to us to give us another chance after we have failed Him so many times. We, in this community are blessed with our churches and the fine Christian members we have in our congregation to make this a happy, growing, harmonious neighborhood.

You set before us an example tonight that I hope each of us can follow in our daily lives. We are indeed grateful to you brother Pastor and friends, for allowing us to come into your hearts tonight and to be a part in this great movement for Christ.

RESPONSE:
We are assured of our welcome here today for you have already shown us your hospitality and we feel humble before the deep friendship you offer us. We feel that the bond between us has already been strengthened. We shall remember these soul-touching words and for days to come will be glad, even glad that we came to your gathering tonight.

We are interested in your church as we are in all churches which work hard for the Founder of the Church, Jesus Christ our Lord. We are grateful to be here and grateful for your words of welcome.

RESPONSE:
Giving Honor to God, the Mistress of Ceremonies, Pastor, Pulpit Guest, and Fellow Christians:

Your heartfelt greeting makes our hearts glad. We appreciate all the kind words and the wonderful welcome you have given us this evening.
We are grateful to you for inviting us and we hope that when we leave you will feel that you have received a blessing from the words we have to say, but most of all from the Christ which we carry in our hearts. You are very kind and very cordial and your kindness and cordiality is deeply appreciated.

RESPONSE:
We the members of _____, are indeed grateful to you tonight for your invitation to such a special occasion and the opportunity to share in its happiness. Your prayers and your songs have been an inspiration to us already and it is with sincere gratitude that we accept your welcome.

In your greetings you have just shown us your love—not for self, but for God and His children and we bask in that love, as flowers bask and bloom in the sunshine.

You have shown your courage by holding forth the word of truth and ever moving forward, onward for God's kingdom.

You have shown your faith—sincere faith in God and His word, by following your usual custom of long-range planning and then carrying through to the desired outcome.

You have shown us your joy, the joy of the Lord is our strength and this joy attracts others out in the world who do not know the happiness of being safe in Jesus.

We are happy Christians tonight and as we worship with you throughout the rest of the program, I pray God's blessing upon every word spoken and everything that is done. May it be done to the glory of God.

"Honored One"

"A gracious woman retaineth honor . . ."

We, the family of Mrs. Louisteen Bolding-Harris have suffered a great loss in her home-going, but truly we appreciate her for always remembering to listen, to understand and to care . . . For always finding time to help, to play or encourage a dream and for never losing the knack of making a child and or student feel special and very much loved!

Indeed the teaching profession, family,
Cuney BTW graduates and students will miss her.
YOUR LOVING MEMORIES LIVE ON IN OUR HEARTS

Chapter 3

Tribute To An Usher—Resolution

Whereas, the Hugo Chapel Baptist Church and/or (Church of Affiliation) has suffered a great loss in the home-going of Brother _____ (Name of Deceased) who was loved by all who knew him. He lived a true Christian life and has served as an usher every since uniting with our church. His loyalty to his church, his faithfulness to his family and his kindness to his friends shall ever be a living memorial to his beautiful life. He has labored hard and long and the Lord has promised him rest.

Whereas, Bro. _____ departed this life (Date of Death) at (Time), and will no longer go about his accustomed duties, we mourn, but not as those who have no hope, but as those who expect to meet with him again in that other world beyond the horizon, therefore;

Be It Resolved, that we strive to emulate his beautiful service filled life in every respect; that we express our sympathy to his sorrowing family and present them a copy of these resolutions with the reminder that Jesus, the Man of Sorrow, understands all that transpires in human experience and that He said, "Come unto me all ye that labor and are heavy laden, and I will give your rest. Matt. 11:28. Also our Lord said, "Blessed are they that mourn for they shall be comforted."

Humbly Submitted—The Hugo Chapel Usher Board
Pastor: _____
Sister Louisteen Harris, President

A RESOLUTION (Written by My Mama):
   We the officers and member of the _____ Church, in sincerity extend our deepest sympathy to *(family)* in this hour of bereavement, caused by the passing of *(deceased name)*.

   In the passing of _____, we sincerely recognize that we have lost a faithful member, an ardent and devout laborer, and a warm and sympathetic friend.

   Resolve, that we, the members of _____ Church, bow in humble submission to the will of God, and commend the bereaved family to Him who sees all and knows every heart. Console yourselves in the hope of a reunion, that after life's remaining ills are past, that it is like healing oil to the wounded heart, comforted with pleasing rather than sad thoughts. Be it further resolved. That we enter sympathetically into the sorrows of the bereaved, and bid them hope, through the Master of all life, that they shall see their loved one again, for the last enemy that shall destroy us is death.

   Then, we shall meet with the loved ones gone. We shall know as we are known, some sweet day, "Bye and Bye."

Humbly submitted;
_____ Pastor
_____ Church Clerk

Patricia L. Harris-Cook, Daughter

The Resolution Of Mrs. Louisteen Bolding-Harris
Hugo Chapel Missionary Baptist Church—Hugo, Oklahoma

Whereas, it has pleased our heavenly Father to translate from the labors of this life to the sweet rest and fellowship of the saints in heaven our dearly beloved sister in the Lord, Mrs. Louisteen Bolding Harris and;

Whereas, we, the members of the Hugo Chapel Missionary Baptist Church desire to place on record our love and esteem for her life and labor; and in view of her noble and sincere testimony which has been an example of Christian womanhood and devotion to the Kingdom's cause, we thank the heavenly Father for her, and feel that we should express our sympathy to her husband, son, and daughter, as well as other relatives and friends.

We thank the Lord for the privilege of having known this fine and spiritual personality, who was so interested in God's work, that she was in attendance at all of the services of her church and enjoyed the full privileges of its membership. She prayed faithfully for her church and her pastor gave them his faithful support at all times.

For more than 40 years when she first allied herself with the Hugo Chapel Missionary Baptist church until September 19, 1993 when the Lord called her home, Mrs. Harris never ceased to show an active interest in the programs of this organization. She served in the Sunday School as Primary Class Teacher, as Usher Board President, Missionary Bible Instructor and Church Clerk. She was ever willing to do her part and cheerfully assumed any responsibility which was hers.

Although she was ever willing to serve, Mrs. Harris never sought a place of prominence. She did everything requested of her, as unto the Lord, but her spirit of genuine humility followed the example of her Lord, making her willing to do the humblest tasks, as well as important ones, doing both well, yet not seeking recognition for the same.

Mrs. Harris truly loved her Lord, serving in many Christian capacities, and it is a small wonder that her unselfish and cooperative nature made for her many friends.

Be it therefore resolved, that though her presence will be greatly missed by her loved ones and those to whom she had endeared herself in our organization, that they accept the Christian submission to God's will, His calling our beloved sister, Mrs. Louisteen Harris home. To her devoted husband, daughter, son and other relatives and friends, we extend our heartfelt sympathy and commend them to the Divine Comforter who is able to sustain, encourage and strengthen all who call upon Him.

Resolve further, that we will ever cherish her memory and emulate her admirable traits, and look forward with joy to meeting her in the home which she knew for so many years was being prepared for her in the Glory-land.

"Precious is the sight of the Lord in the death of His saints. For whether we die, we die unto the Lord; whether we live therefore, or die, we are the Lord's."

                Lovingly submitted:

                Rev. Roylia Akins, Pastor
                Sis. Johnnye Stewart, Church Clerk,
                Hugo Chapel Missionary Baptist Church
                Hugo, Oklahoma

Obituaries

An OBITUARY; written by My Mama:

"For me to live is Christ, and to die is gain," said the apostle Paul. We know that this would be the message if our dear Sister and/or/Brother were able to give us a message today from the portals of heaven where she/he has gone to be forever with the Lord. It is said that Fanny Crosby, the great hymn writer, on her death bed said, "How can anyone call it a dark valley? It is all Light and Love!" Then stretching her arms out to Christ, she whispered, "I could run to meet Him." This Christian woman/man whom we memorialize today must have felt the same way for she/he loved the Lord, and always wanted others to know.

To his Thessalonians friends, Paul wrote, "I would not have you to be ignorant, brethren, concerning them which are asleep, that ye sorrow not, even as others which have no hope." (I Thessalonians 4:13). Hope of what? What possible hope can bring comfort at such a time as this when we morn the passing of so dear a woman/man, so great a leader?

In "the first dark days of nothingness" or still darker days which follow, listen, and thank God with all your heart for every word from the Scriptures, "For if we believe that Jesus died and rose again, even so then those also which sleep in Jesus will God bring with Him." (I Thes. 4:14).

The dear face, for the sight of which we hunger shall look on us again; the voice that has left this world so tuneless shall once more bless our ears; we shall see our loved one again and be with forevermore!

"There's an open gate at the end of the road—through which each must go alone, and there, in light we cannot see Our Father claims His own. Beyond the gate your love one finds happiness and rest, and there is comfort in the thought that a loving God knows best."

Rules and By-Laws for Usher's/Nurse's Unit
At the Hugo Chapel Baptist Church

As a dedicated Church Usher for over 30 years my mama loved her Church. These are Rules and Regulation written for Ushers/Nurse's with the consent of the Board:

1. The time of each meeting will be *(day)* before the first and third Sunday at *(time)* for adults. Young People will meet ***(day)/(time)*** before the first and third Sunday.
2. Dues will be $1.00 for adults monthly and .50 cent for children.
3. All members are asked to please be on time for all meetings and duties. Anyone who is unable to attend should call the nursing supervisor or the president.
4. All members that are ill should be sent a get well card.
5. The president should open all meetings on time.
6. Meetings should be kept in order at all times. (No talking).
7. All members are to be neat and in uniform for duty. Nurses will wear white uniforms, white shoes, white hose, and white nurses' caps. Ushers uniform per direction of the president.
8. Do not chew gum in meetings or while on duty.
9. Always be alert in meetings or on duty.
10. All members are to love each other, and be kind to one another.
11. A Bible verse is to be said when paying dues.
12. Open and close meetings with a song and prayer

Usher Theme: "Love One Another"

Closing: "May the Lord watch between me and thee, when we are absent one from another." Genesis 31:49.

Patricia L. Harris-Cook, Daughter

In Memory of My Mama
Mrs. Louisteen Harris

Yours was a useful life;
You wrought well while here.
You were generous with your time,
As you toiled from year to year.
Many a life you did touch,
Always doing your part.
Glad to serve when called upon.
With a meek and humble heart.
Your life was dedicated
To things noble and true.
It was no task for you to work
That, you wanted to do!
Through you have passed away,
The deeds you have left behind
Will live on each day.
We didn't want to give you up . . .
Sleep, sleep on, take your rest.
This act of God we dare not question,
For He alone, knows best.

(Author Unknown)

Chapter 4

Words of Wisdom

Mission Lesson [Notes]—"Called Out Redemption"

2 Tim. 1:9 "Who has saved us, and called us with a holy calling, not according to our works, but according to his own purpose and grace, which was given us in Christ Jesus before the world began."

Romans 8:6-11
- 6> For to be carnally minded is death; but to be spiritually minded is life and peace.
- 7> Because the carnal mind is enmity against God: for it is not subject to the law of God, neither indeed can be.
- 8> So then they that are in the flesh cannot please God.
- 9> But ye are not in the flesh, but in the Spirit, if so be that the Spirit of God dwell in you. Now if any man have not the Spirit of Christ, he is none of his.
- 10> Any if Christ be in you, the body is dead because of sin; but the Spirit is life because of righteousness.
- 11> But the Spirit of him that raised up Jesus from the dead dwell in you, he that raised up Christ from the dead shall also quicken your mortal bodies by his Spirit that dwelleth in you.

I Peter 1:14-15
- 14> As obedient children, not fashioning yourselves according to the former lusts in your ignorance:

15> But as he which hast called you is holy, so be ye holy in all manner of conversation.

Romans 12:1 "I beseech you therefore, brethren, by the mercies of God, that ye present your bodies a living sacrifice, holy, acceptable unto God, which is your reasonable service."

Romans 6:4 "Therefore we are buried with him by baptism into death: that like as Christ was raised up from the dead by the glory of the Father, even so we also should walk in the newness of life."

Psalms 136:1-6 "O Give Thanks"
- 1> O Give thanks unto the Lord; for he is good: for his mercy endureth for ever.
- 2> O give thanks unto the God of gods: for his mercy endureth for ever.
- 3> O give thanks to the Lord of lords: for his mercy endureth for ever.
- 4> To him who alone doeth great wonders: for his mercy endureth forever.
- 5> To him that by wisdom made the heavens: for his mercy endureth for ever.
- 6> To him that stretched out the earth above the waters: for his mercy endureth for ever.

(King James Version)
WORD'S AND VERSES FOR WISDOM

FLOOD STAGE:
Because we are descendants of Abraham, we can get into the Flood stage of blessings by our faith in God. To be constantly on the winning side, we must "stay" with God or else we will become as Israel—a defeated people.

NOBODY'S FRIEND

My name is **Gossip**. I have not respect for justice
I maim without killing. I break hearts and ruin lives
I am cunning and malicious and gather strength with age.
The more I am quoted the more I am believed
My victims are helpless.
They cannot protect themselves against me because
I have no name and no face.
To track me down is impossible.
The harder you try, the more elusive I become.
I am nobody's friend.
Once I tarnish a reputation, it is never the same.
I topple governments and wreck marriages.
I ruin careers and cause sleepless nights,
heartaches and indigestion.
I make innocent people cry in their pillows.
Even my name hisses. I am called Gossip.
I make headlines and headaches.
Before you repeat a story, ask yourself:
It is true? Is it harmless? Is it necessary?
If is isn't . . . DON'T REPEAT.

A Journey of Faith and Miracles

If we obey God and make Him our Source, give tithes of all,
we will be healed of all diseases and blessed spiritually,
financially, etc. Withholding from God prevents our miracles.
We cannot live without God as our Source.

Jesus told his disciples that others would be able to identify them as His followers by the love that they showed to one another. Can we measure up as Christians with that same yardstick? If we were brought to trial and accused of being followers of Christ, would there be enough evidence to convict us? Jesus showed us how to love by the way He lived and the way He Died. Come and learn more about His love and how it can transform your life, in the church of your choice.

Chapter 5

My Mama's Notes On Great Scriptures In The Word Of God

Exodus 20:1-17	The Ten Commandments
St. Mark 12:28-31	The first and second commandments, the greatest commandments.
St. Luke 6:38	"Give, and it shall be given unto you; good measure, pressed down, shaken together, and running over will be put into your bosom. For with the same measure that you use, it will be measured back to you."
Luke 11:2-4	The Lord's Prayer
Matthew 6:9-13	The Lord's Prayer
Matthew 5:3-12	The Beatitudes
Psalms 23	A Psalm of David: Confidence in God' Grace
Matthew 5, 6, 7	The Sermon on the Mount
John 3:16	The golden text of the Bible; "God so loved the world . . ."
Ephesians 2:8} Ephesians 4:7} Habakkuk 2:4}	Grace is available
Romans 1:17 } Galatians 3:11 } Hebrews 10:38 }	The just shall live by faith

Luke 4:18	Jesus' Mission
II Timothy 2:15	"Study to show thyself approved unto God," etc.
John 11:1-45	Jesus raises Lazarus
John 11:35	The shortest verse: "Jesus Wept."
Isaiah 53:	The suffering of the Lord
Luke 10:2	The Harvest truly is great, but the laborers few.
Malachi 2:8-10}	
Luke 18:12}	
I Corinthians 16:1-2}	About Tithing
II Corinthians 9:6-8}	
Hebrews 7:6}	
John 17	The prayer Jesus prayed
Luke 19:1-10	Jesus grants Zacchaeus salvation
John 10:1-17	Jesus, the good shepherd
John 15:3-7	Parable of the Lost Sheep
Luke 17:11-19	Jesus cleanses ten (10) lepers
Hebrews 11:1	Definition of faith

The Books of the Bible: *Mama's Memo's*

Being the Bible scholar that 'My Mama' was, she always wrote down things she wanted to remember for future references, and to mediate upon. My Mama also wrote down scriptures and writings when she sought knowledge and greater understanding of the word of God.

The books of the Bible are listed in her journal with notations beside each. After reading her journal, I decided to share with readers her intense love of the scriptures and her interpretations of the Books of the Bible.

Note: Be reminded that my mother was very ill during these writings—her hand writing was a little distorted. I feel that within her mind, she was preparing for her death. Source from which references were found, unknown.

THE OLD TESTAMENT

Genesis   -The Seed of the Woman
Exodus   -He is our Passover Lamb

Leviticus	-He is our High Priest
Numbers	-He is the pillar of cloud by day, and the pillar of fire by night.
Deuteronomy	-He is the Prophet like unto Moses
Joshua	-He is the Captain of our salvation
Judges	-He is our Judge and Law Giver
Ruth	-He is our Kinsman Redeemer
I-II Samuel	-He is our Trusted Prophet
I-II Kings	-He is Our Reigning King
I-II Chronicles	-He is Our Reigning King
Ezra	-He is our Faithful Scribe
Nehemiah	-He is the re-builder of the broken down walls of Human Life
Ester	-He is our Mordecai
Job	-He is our Ever Living Redeemer 'For I know my Redeemer Lives.'
Psalms	-Our Shepherd
Proverbs	-He is our Wisdom
Ecclesiastes*Song of Solomon*Isaiah*Jeremiah	*(No references)*
Lamentation	-He is our Weeping Prophet
Ezekiel*Daniel	*(No references)*
Hosea	-He is our Faithful Husband, forever married to the backslider
Joel	-He is the Baptizer with the Holy Ghost and Fire.
Amos	-He is our Burden Bearer
Obadiah	-He is the Mighty to Save
Jonah	-He is our Great Foreign Missionary He is the Mighty to Save.
Micah	-He is the Messenger with beautiful Feet.
Nahum	-Habakkuk-Zephaniah-Haggai-Zechariah *(No References)*

THE NEW TESTAMENT

Matthew:	-He is Messiah ~ Our Messiah
Mark:	-He is the Wonder Worker
Luke:	-He is the Son of Man
John:	-He is the Son of God

The Acts:	-He is the Holy Ghost
Epistle to the Romans:	-He is the Holy Ghost
I &II Corinthians:	-He is the Sanctifier (Our) Sanctifier
Galatians:	-He is the Redeemer from the Curse of the Law
Ephesians:	-He is the Christ of Unsearchable Riches
Philippians:	*(No References)*
Colossians:	-He is the Father of the Godhead
I-II Thessalonians:	-He is our Soon Coming King
I-II Timothy:	-He is our Mediator between God and Man
Titus:	-Bodily—He is our Faithful Pastor
Philemon:	-He is our Friend that Sticketh Closer than a Brother.
To the Hebrews:	-He is our Wisdom ~ He is Covenant
Epistle of James:	-He is our Great Physician and the Prayer of Faith Shall Save the Sick.
I-II Peter	*(No References)*
I /II/III John:	-He Is Love.
Jude:	-He is the Lord Coming with Ten Thousand of His Saints
	The Blood of the Everlasting
Revelation:	-He is King of kings and Lord of lords.

He Is . . .
Abel's Sacrifice
Noah's Rainbow
Abraham's Ram
Jacob's Ladder
Moses' Rod
Isaac's Wells
Elisha's Staff
David's Slingshot
Amos's Burden
Daniel's Visions
Peter's Shadow
Stephen's Signs and Wonders
Paul's Handkerchief

18 Parables

1. Matthew 13:24-30 — Enemy who sowed a mite
2. Matthew 13:31-33 — Mustard seed and leaven
3. Matthew 18:25-35 — Unmerciful debtor
4. Matthew 20:1-16 — Laborer in the vineyard
5. Matthew 21:34-41 — Parable of the vineyard
6. Matthew 22:1-14 — Parable of wedding feast
7. Matthew 25:1-13 — Parable of the ten (10) virgins
8. Matthew 25:14-30 — Parable of the talents
9. Matthew 25:31-46 — Jesus describes the "Last Judgment"
10. Mark 4:1-9 — Parable of the soil (sower)
11. Mark 12:1-12 — Ungrateful husbandmen
12. Luke 10:30:37 — Parable of good Samaritan
13. Luke 12:16-31 — Parable of rich "fool"
14. Luke 14:15-24 — Parable of great supper
15. Luke 19:11-27 — Parable of the ten (10) pounds
16. Luke 15:8-10 — Parable of the lost coin
17. Luke 15:11-32 — Parable of prodigal son
18. Luke 18:9-14 — Parable of Pharisee Publican (Tax Collector)

Blessed Assurance Scriptures

John 16:13	Believe in Spirit and truth
James 1:18	Believe in Gods words (truth)
I Timothy 2:11-12	Women should be silent in church
I Corinthians 11:14-15	About long hair
I Corinthians 11:3-13	About wearing hats in church
Mark 25:25	The hour when Jesus was crucified.
Mark 15:33	The hours when darkness was over the land, when Jesus was crucified.
Mark 15:34	Jesus' greatest suffering
Acts 2:1-4	Pentecost: Peter preached the sermon
Romans 3:23	For all have sinned.
III John V.2	"God expects us all to be in good health."
Proverbs 31:10:31	Qualities of a good wife
John 19:26	Jesus' beloved disciple
Luke 1:50	God has mercy on us
Acts 9	Conversion of Paul
John 14	Remarks of Jesus—said before His crucifixion
Mark 9:1-10	Transfiguration of Jesus
John 3:1-13	Nicodemus and Jesus

Acts 12:1-2	"Herod kills James," the only disciple killed.
Luke 2:1-20	Birth of Jesus Christ
Matthew 1:18-25	Birth of Jesus Christ
Mark 11:12-14	The only miracle of destruction by Jesus-the Fig Tree.
Isaiah 11:6	The leopard shall lie down with the kid.
Mark 15:37	Jesus gave up the ghost.
Mark 1:9	John the Baptist baptized Jesus
John 3:22} John 4:1 }	Jesus baptized
Matthew 19:3-9	Jesus speaks concerning divorce.
Mark 1:22, 27	Jesus' authority
John 9:1-12	Jesus heals a man born blind
Jeremiah 36	The Bible is indispensable, it will not be destroyed.
Mark 2:23-28} Mark 3:1-6 }	Religion can be vital
Mark 10:35-45	Way of unselfish service
Luke 11:1-13	Way of Genuine Prayer
Mark 5:21-43	Power over sickness and death
Matthew 19:26	All things are possible with God
John 16:13	Believe in the Spirit and truth

James 1:18	Believe in Gods words (truth)
1 Corinthians 7:19	ABOUT CIRCUMCISION:

Circumcision is nothing, and uncircumcision is nothing, but keeping the commandments of God is what matters.

Matthew 28:18-20	The Great Commission
Matthew 28 } Mark 16 } Luke 24 } St. John 20 }	The Resurrection
Revelation 21, 22	The New Heaven
Romans 3	What is wrong with us?
John 3	Remedy for us
John 15:	The Vine Chapter—(Abiding Chapter)
I Corinthians 13	The Love Chapter—(Faith, Hope, and Charity these 3)
I Thessalonians 5} 1 Corinthians } The Revelation }	Jesus' Second Coming
Matthew 7:7	Ask, and it shall be given you, seek and ye shall find.
John 4:1-19	Jesus and the woman of Samaria at the well.
Matthew 28:19	The three in one; (Father, Son and Holy Ghost)
Matthew 18:15	If thy Brother trespass against thee.
Matthew 18:20	"For where two or three are gathered together in My name, I am there in the midst of them."
Matthew 19:16-19	To have eternal life.
Matthew 21:1-11	Jesus triumphal entry into Jerusalem.

Matthew 21:12-13	Jesus drives money changers from the temple.
Luke 23:50-56	Joseph of Arimathea request body of Jesus. (Burial)
John 6:71-72	Jesus calls Judas a devil
Luke 2:7-16	Birth of Jesus—Shepherds told, by angel
Matthew 2:1-11	Birth of Jesus; Story of Wise men
Matthew 14:15-21	Jesus feeds five thousand (5,000)
Matthew 14:22-33	Jesus walks on the water
Matthew 6:25-34	Don't worry
Luke 2:31-52	The boy, Jesus in the temple
Matthew 14:1-12	John the Baptist—beheaded
Luke 2:25-35	Simon sees Christ
Luke 4:16-32	Jesus read scripture in Church
Luke 4:18	Jesus' Mission

Chapter 6

Speeches

By: My Mama; Mrs. Louisteen Bolding-Harris

"The Importance of a Beautiful Tongue"

Pastor _____, Pulpit guest(s), our gracious Mistress of Ceremonies, Christian workers and friends.

'The Importance of a Beautiful Tongue'
   How beautiful is your tongue? Or haven't you ever really considered your tongue in terms of its attractiveness?
   You don't look at it very often in the mirror. You don't go on shopping trips for it. You don't have a weekly appointment at the tongue beautician.
   Avon and Revlon don't sell cosmetics for it. You don't have to diet to get it back in shape . . . Yet, it is your tongue, more than the form of your face or the dimensions of your figure or the lavishness of your wardrobe, or the size of your income which determines whether or not you are a beautiful person. King Solomon was by no means a Puritan in his judgments on beauty, yet in his poem, Song of Solomon he pays tribute to the beauty of the tongue. "Your lips are like a scarlet thread, and your words are delightful." (The Song of Solomon 4:3)
   The tongue can give new delights year after year. The tongue can make a plain person into a beautiful person. The tongue can heal bruises and scrapes. The tongue can soothe the agitated temper. It can give hope to the

despondent soul. The tongue can point the way to God. The Bible compares it to the rudder of a ship—which although it is relatively small, controls the direction of the entire vessel.

"Look at the ships also; though they are so great and are driven by strong winds. They are guided by a very small rudder wherever the will of the pilot directs." (James 3:4)

The Bible also compares the tongue to a fire—of which a small spark can create a great holocaust. "So the tongue is a little member and boasts of great things. How great a forest is set ablaze by a small fire" (James 3:5).

The tongue can make or break your marriage. It can make your home a paradise or a desert. It can draw your children to you in affection or send them away in disgust.

It can make and keep friends or lose them. It can defend a good cause or allow an evil cause to go unchecked. It can make the difference between hiring and firing. It can heal a church or kill it. It can attract people to Christ or send them away from Him. It can honor God or dishonor Him. It can save potential suicides, and it can drive people to self destruction. As Proverbs 18:21 says, "Death and life are in the power of the tongue."

Your reputation will, in large part, be established by the use you make of your tongue. It will leave a lasting impression on people. Your tongue will label your character. The bystanders at the trial of Jesus said more than they realized when they said to Peter, "Your accent betrays you." (Matthew 26:73)

It's not an easy matter to cultivate an attractive tongue. Every kind of beast and bird, and reptile and sea creature, can be tamed and has been tamed by humankind, but no human being can tame the tongue.

James 3:7, 8 says, "It is a restless evil full of deadly poison. The tongue is an ornery critter, wild as a bucking bronco. Just when we think we have it under control—its mighty energy harnessed, its wild nature tamed—the wild Mustang spirit breaks out again, sending the snorting creature into a bucking spree.

How then can the tongue be tamed?

This powerful organ can be made beautiful and powerful only by bringing it under the control of an even greater power—the Power of God's Holy Spirit.

Jesus promised, "you shall receive power when the Holy Spirit has come upon you." (Acts 1:8) When the Spirit came at Pentecost, the first object on earth that it used was the tongue! The disciples began to speak in languages that could be understood by the foreign Jews who were visiting in Jerusalem for the feast. Simon Peter—the same Peter who had earlier cursed and sworn before a servant girl while denying Christ—got up to give a sermon, and the Holy Spirit used his tongue so marvelously that three thousand people responded and were saved.

In I Corinthians 12:3 we read, "Therefore I want you to understand that no one speaking by the Spirit of God ever says, "Jesus be cursed!" "And no one can say "Jesus is Lord" except by the Holy Spirit." It is the Spirit which transforms the cursing tongue into a confessing tongue.

The conclusion of the matter is this: Your tongue cannot become a thing of beauty by your own efforts alone. It takes the superhuman work of the Holy Spirit.

This is not to say that your own effort is not needed. God has given you a mind and a will, and He expects you to use them.

He requires that you assume responsibility over the marvelous instrument He has given you. He has revealed a wealth of information and advice on how to use the tongue and He expects us to put it into practice.

Include in your prayers a few sincere petitions for that important piece of flesh which lies between your teeth. Recognize that it is the Holy Spirit who can give it both discipline and power. Begin to yield your tongue to that Spirit.

The Human Tongue Is Distinctive. Some animals have fancier tongues than humans do. Snakes and lizards have forked tongues which also serve as organs of smell.

Frogs and toads have very long tongues which can dart out with blinding speed to capture insects. Although our human tongue cannot harpoon a dinner, bite or smell, they can do something even more fantastic—they can form words. This is one of the abilities which makes us distinctive from the animal world, and this is one of the abilities which gives us such a tremendous potential for both good and evil.

Isaiah's Tongue: Isaiah 6:1 relates the story of how God called Isaiah to become a prophet. He did so by first giving him a vision of his awesome holiness and then sanctifying the prophet's tongue. Isaiah realized, after catching a glimpse of the purity of God, that his tongue needed to be purified and He said, "Woe is me! For I am lost; for I am a man of unclean lips, and I dwell in the midst of a people of unclean lips. (V.5) The angel touched the prophet's lips with a burning coal taken from the fire—a token of forgiveness and restoration (and perhaps a hint about how painful it is to cleanse the tongue). "Behold, this has touched your lips, your guilt is taken away, and your sin is forgiven." (V.7) . . . Then and only then was Isaiah ready for service; (V.8) "And I heard the voice of the Lord saying, "Whom shall I send, and who will go for us?" Then I said, "Here am I! Send me." When we become aware of the holiness of God, we become aware of how much our tongues need to be cleansed.

In order to be ready to serve we must let God cleanse our tongues.

* * *

Speech: "Education—A Privilege"

Education is truly the greatest privilege ever known to any civilization. It is in education that America has put her trust.

The founding fathers of our magnificent and splendid United States firmly believed that education was the key to unlock the hidden treasures of the vast universe. Their belief has become a reality, for education has demonstrated to all mankind that it is the essential tool with which every worthwhile endeavor is accomplished.

In Colonial America education was highly prized by the colonist for it promised to bring to real life the American dream of the good society.

In the present age, education is considered the most valuable possession attainable. It places one in a more favorable position on the social ladder of success. Likewise it rewards one with a higher income in which to purchase the luxuries of good living. Lastly, an education creates within a person the feeling of self satisfaction in a job well done.

The World Book Encyclopedia Dictionary defines a privilege as a special right given to a person as a favor due him because of his position, age, sex, citizenship, etc.

Ladies, gentlemen, and fellow citizens, education is indeed a special privilege. Mere words could never express my appreciation to every citizen, both living and dead, who made it possible for me to receive a highly prized gift—A Good Education.

Education is a gigantic enterprise. There are approximately 37,000,000 people (1970) of the United States enrolled in kindergarten through the university. More than 1,243,000 teachers are employed (1970) in public and private schools. The total cost of education yearly is roughly estimated at nine million. (1970).

The aspirations, ideals, purposes and goals of America are expressed through education.

The future of our country is vitally involved in education. The challenge is to every citizen to preserve, to exalt, to enrich and to cherish education.

Speech: "A Pattern of Thinking—The 23rd Psalms"

The 23rd Psalms is a pattern of thinking and when a mind becomes saturated with it, a new way of thinking and a new life are the result.

This Psalms is prescribed as follows: Read it 5 (five) times a day, for 7 (seven) days. Read it carefully and prayerfully—and at the end of one week . . . A new way of thinking will be deeply and firmly implanted within your mind that will bring marvelous changes in your thinking and give you a new life.

THE LORD IS MY SHEPHERD: I SHALL NOT WANT:

Think of God as our Shepherd. The sheep knows that the shepherd made ample provision for it today, so will he tomorrow. As Christians we have assurance that we shall not want for food, we shall not want for shelter, we shall not want for clothing—we shall not want for anything—for God shall abundantly supply our needs. All life came from God. That includes my life. God keeps faith with fowls of the air and the grass of the field. And Jesus asks us to think that if God will do so much for a simple bird or a wild flower how much more will He do for us?

HE MAKETH ME TO LIE DOWN IN GREEN PASTURES:

The shepherd starts the sheep grazing about 4 A.M. The sheep walk steadily as they are grazing. They are never still. By 10 A.M., the sun is beaming down, the sheep are hot, tired and thirsty. The wise Shepherd knows the sheep must not drink when it is HOT. Neither when its stomach is filled—so the shepherd makes the sheep lie down in green pastures, in a cool, soft spot.

Sometimes it takes sickness to make us lie down. Often God puts us on our backs, in order to give us a chance to look up.

Study the lives of great people, and you will find that every one of them drew apart from the hurry and scurry of life for rest and reflection.

Many times we are forced, not by God, but by circumstances to lie down. That can always be a blessing. Even the bed of an invalid may be a blessing if he takes advantage of it.

Mr. Whittier so eloquently sums it up as follows: "Take from our souls the strain and stress and let our ordered lives confess The beauty of Thy Peace."

HE LEADETH ME BESIDE THE STILL WATERS:

The sheep is a very timid creature. Especially is it afraid of swiftly moving water. The shepherd knows about this fear. He does not laugh nor does he try to force the sheep. Instead, he leads his sheep across the mountains and valleys. He is constantly on the watch for still waters where the thirst of the sheep may be quenched.

God knows our limitations, yet He does not condemn us for our weakness.

He does not force us where we cannot safely and happily go. God never demands of us work which is beyond our strength and abilities.

HE RESTORETH MY SOUL:

As the sheep start out in the morning each one takes a definite place in line. However, some time during the day, each sheep leaves its place in line and trots over to the Shepherd. The shepherd gently rubs the nose, lightly scratches the ears, and pats the sheep. Reassured and encouraged the sheep takes its place in line again.

David remembered how close he once was to God, how God protected him as he went out to meet the giant Goliath, how God guided him along the way to success. Then David got busy. He was able to look after himself. He felt no need of God. He lost his nearness to God. He did wrong. Thus, David became unhappy. His burden of guilt became too heavy to bear. He repented. God heard, forgave, and restored. He became a NEW MAN. When David said, 'He restoreth my soul,' in essence, he meant—He revives life in me.

HE LEADETH ME IN THE PATH OF RIGHTEOUSNESS FOR HIS NAME'S SAKE:

Doubtless, David remembered his own experience as a shepherd. He knew that the sheep had no sense of direction. He knew of their poor vision—for a sheep cannot see 10 or 15 yards ahead. In Palestine, the fields were covered with narrow paths over which the shepherds led their sheep to pasture. Some of these paths led up a blind alley. But some paths led to green pastures and still waters. The sheep obediently followed the shepherd, knowing it was walking in the right path.

Often we come to the forks of life's road and cannot decide which way to turn. If we put our trust in God—He will lead and direct us in the right path.

YEA THOUGH I WALK THROUGH THE VALLEY OF THE SHADOW OF DEATH—I WILL FEAR NO EVIL; FOR THOU ART WITH ME:

"The valley of the shadow of death" refers to more than the actual experience of death. It has been translated "the glen of gloom." It may refer to every hard and terrifying experience of life.

The Sheepherder describes an actual Valley of the Shadow of Death in Palestine. It leads from Jerusalem to the Dead Sea, and is a very narrow and dangerous pathway through the mountain range. The path is rough and there is danger that a sheep may fall at any moment to its death.

Although this is a dangerous journey, the sheep is not afraid; Why? Because the shepherd is leading and guiding it.

And so come those dark places in life through which we are compelled to pass. Death is one. Disappointment is another. Loneliness another. There are many more. In these valleys—quit struggling for a while. STOP; become still and quiet, and in the midst of your "glen of gloom" you will feel a strange and marvelous presence, more powerfully than you have ever felt before.

David said, "Wherever my pathway leads, I will not be afraid." Why?

FOR THOU ART WITH ME. THY ROD AND THY STAFF THEY COMFORT ME:

The sheep is a helpless animal. It has no weapon with which to fight. It is easy prey to any wild beast of the field. How is he comforted? The shepherd carries a rod two or three feet long. When David wrote this Psalms—no doubt—he remembered his own need for such a rod. For in I Samuel 17, he tells Saul how he slew a lion and a bear while protecting his sheep.

The Shepherd also has another weapon—a staff about 8 feet long. The end of the staff was turned into a crook. Many paths in Palestine were along the steep sides of mountains. The sheep would lose its footing and slip down, hanging hopelessly on some ledge below.

With the staff, the shepherd could reach down—place the crook over the chest of the sheep—and lift it back onto the pathway. It is comforting to the sheep to know that the shepherd will be able to meet an emergency.

Seemingly there is overwhelming evil in the world. We are a frightened people. Many times we feel helpless; then we find comfort in realizing the power of God. "Thy rod and thy staff" takes a lot of dread and fear of the future out of our hearts.

THOU PREPARETH A TABLE BEFORE ME IN THE PRESENCE OF MINE ENEMIES:

Poisonous plants grew in the pastures of the Holy Land. Each spring, the Shepherd would take these poisonous plants out and burn them: thereby making the pastures safe for the sheep to graze. The pastures became a prepared table. The present enemies were destroyed.

As we move along through life, there will be varied forms of enemies seeking to destroy us, but God will shield us from all evil and provide us with ample food to nourish our bodies.

THOU ANOINTEST MY HEAD WITH OIL; MY CUP RUNNETH OVER:

Sometimes as the sheep grazed, its head would be cut by the sharp edge of a stone buried in the grass. Also, there were briars to scratch and thorns to stick.

So the Shepherd—at the end of the day examined each sheep. If there were hurt places, the shepherd would apply soothing and healing oil. From a huge earthen jug of refreshing, cool water, each sheep was given a cup, brimful of water. The tired animal drank deeply.

As Christians, often the burden of daily living seems unbearable. Sometimes our hearts are broken; feeling are hurt. The world may deal cruelly and harshly, but *HOW SWEET IT IS TO KNOW THAT GOD CAN HEAL ALL OUR ACHES.* He will fill our "cup" with happiness until it overflows.

Begin tomorrow with hope, plant this firmly in your mind, "Surely goodness and mercy shall follow me . . ."

AND I WILL DWELL IN THE HOUSE OF THE LORD FOREVER:

Just knowing intimately a God like he describes in the 23rd Psalms gave David assurance that at the close of life's day he would go home. That is the hope of all Christians to go home and live eternally with God.

(Thank you for your time and attention).

Chapter 7

Readings

The Lord's Prayer

There was one thing about Jesus that stood out to His disciples and that was his prayer life. They noticed when Jesus prayed that something happened! Now it wasn't like that when they prayed—something might or might not happen. There was something about Jesus' prayer that got the desired results. Deeply impressed by the way He prayed the disciples eagerly came to Jesus and said: "Teach us to pray." And Jesus began by saying: After this manner therefore pray ye. Now Jesus was not indicating that this was to be the disciples' sole prayer . . . or that those were to be the only words they were ever to say in prayer. It was not to be a substitute for their prayers. But Jesus meant that they were to pray after the fashion of this particular prayer, which we today call "The Lord's Prayer."

"Let's stand and pray in unison:"
Our Father which art in heaven, Hallowed be thy name. Thy kingdom come, Thy will be done in earth, as it is in heaven. Give us this day our daily bread. And forgive us our trespasses as we forgive those who trespass against us.
And lead us not into temptation, but deliver us from evil: For thine is the kingdom, and the Power, and the glory, for ever. Amen.
(Be seated)

OUR FATHER . . .

Jesus began the prayer with "Our Father" . . . The word "Father" as it pertains to God was first used in a personal way by our Lord Jesus Christ. The term Father signified the closeness they had together. It meant that He and God the Father were intimately and personally related. He admonishes us to call God, Father, suggesting the closeness of our relationship with Him.

I'm sure you all are aware of the love and devotion you have for your earthly father. He stands for affection . . . for confidence . . . for protection . . . for love. Think of the times you were ill and how much a word of hope made you feel better. Think of the times you were depressed and your father cheered you up. Think of the many failures you had; yet your father encouraged you to never give up. Think of the times you were disappointed, and your father gave you encouragement.

Papa! Jesus was saying to you and me. "When you pray say, Our Father . . . Our Papa . . . Our Daddy."

WHICH ART . . .

God is. Jesus said when you pray, pray to someone who is . . . Who never changes. The weather changes . . . people change . . . circumstances change . . . but God never changes. God exists . . . HE IS. God Is! God is in your total life—physical, material, and spiritual. You have a 7 day-a-week life . . . 7 day-a-week needs . . . and, a 7 day-a-week God.

God is with you every moment, everyday, every where. God Is!

IN HEAVEN . . .

Now Jesus was not trying to locate God. He was using this term to express the ability and power of God to take care of us and our needs.

When Jesus spoke those words the world was filled with impossibilities all around Him, Jesus saw people hemmed in by circumstances, disease, discrimination, poverty, fear, and failure. And He knew that in Heaven there were resources for man's needs; water for his thirst . . . food for his hunger . . . strength for his weakness . . . riches for his poverty . . . a kiss for his sorrow . . . gladness for his misery . . . and love for his loneliness . . .

Jesus came with outstretched hands filled with God's blessings. He came into people's lives at the point of their need, performing miracles and setting them free.

So Jesus tells us that when we pray to remember that God—Our Father is in HEAVEN. And In Heaven there is no shortage of any good thing. God's riches are laid end-to-end across Heaven waiting to be given to us.

HALLOWED BE THY NAME . . .

Jesus had a deep feeling about the name of God. He never used it irrelevantly . . . nor in vain . . . nor as an obscenity. He reverenced the name of the Father with great honor and love. And He said to you and to me, "When you pray, be sure that you have reverence for the name of God.

Note: Optional; Tell Story about the famous photographer, at end of this reading

THY KINGDOM COME . . .

Jesus was very concerned about the nations . . . the kingdoms . . . that existed on the earth. But He was more concerned about another kingdom . . . A higher kingdom . . . God's kingdom. And He taught us to pray—". . . thy kingdom come."

We live in earthly kingdoms. These kingdoms are only going to be so powerful—they are limited.

Jesus lived in the Roman Empire, a kingdom of men that had spread over the then—known world. It had conquered the nations and had control over all the people who lived in them. But Jesus said these kingdoms of men are not going to fully conquer everybody . . . these earthly kingdoms are not going to get any bigger, but God's kingdom is . . . and through Him we will get bigger too.

THY WILL BE DONE IN EARTH AS IT IS IN HEAVEN . . .

Every time you pray this, you are praying a revolutionary, radical prayer. You are praying for a new kind of Kingdom to come into being. You are praying that what is IN HEAVEN will come to be . . . down here IN THE EARTH. And that starts with you, with repentance and love. The will of God starts in Heaven but it must be lived in this earthen vessel. This affects you where you are and as you are.

GIVE US THIS DAY OUR DAILY BREAD . . .

When Jesus said, "Give us this day our daily bread," He meant "Give us this day our material needs." Jesus knew all about physical necessities of life. He knew the worth of the widow's mite. He knew about clothes that needed mending and about not having a place to sleep at night.

Even after His resurrection He showed concern for the Disciples' physical needs.

The day He walked home with two of His friends He sat down at the table and broke bread with them. Several days later when the disciples had been out fishing, Jesus knew they would be hungry, so He prepared food for them.

The only true bread, the only true supply of our material needs, comes through God.

Jesus is talking about bread . . . about God's Bread. He's talking about a supply of our needs that really satisfies . . . about clothes that satisfy . . . an automobile that works . . . a house that becomes a home. God is concerned about your bread. He's concerned about money you need. He's concerned about your physical health. God wants you to have peace. He wants you to live out your days in health and happiness.

FORGIVE US OUR TRESPASSES AS WE FORGIVE THOSE WHO TRESPASS AGAINST US . . .

Jesus indicated that the human race is guilty of trespasses . . . We are debtors. Each of us is a trespasser. We do things we ought not to do . . .

We say things we should not say . . . we think things we should not think.

We are trespassers and our forgiveness must come from God. Men may or may not forgive us, but God will forgive.

A man once said to John Wesley, "I'll never forgive." Wesley replied, "Then pray that you will never sin."

In other words, the only way you are ever going to be forgiven by God of your own trespasses is to forgive the one who trespasses against you.

LEAD US NOT INTO TEMPTATION, BUT DELIVER US FROM EVIL . . .
Jesus is saying "God don't forsake us when the going gets rough. Don't let us get into situations that are bigger than we are. Don't let us get into water over our heads."

FOR THINE IS THE KINGDOM, AND THE POWER, AND THE GLORY, FOREVER—AMEN.

When Jesus said these words He was living in an outpost of the Roman Empire. The Roman soldiers in their barbaric cruelty were everywhere putting their burdens on the people. They were acting like they were going to rule forever . . . that Rome would always be the Master Kingdom. But Jesus looked beyond Rome . . . beyond every other kingdom that would arise on the earth . . . and He said, ". . . Thine is the Kingdom."

Jesus was saying there is something bigger and better and more stable than this or any other earthly kingdom . . . and that kingdom is ruled by the King of kings and the Lord of lords.

You are surrounded by the Kingdom of God . . . an incomparable power that can set you free . . . a glory that can fill your soul. So why settle?

*** *Once upon a time there was a famous photographer* . . .**
This photographer worked for "The Tulsa Daily World Newspaper."
He cursed and would often take the name of the Lord in vain. His wife, a Christian, after taking it as long as she could—told him, "Don't you ever curse the name of my Lord in my presence again. Moreover, she said God changed my life. Although I love you, Jesus of Nazareth means more to me and He has done more for me than anyone else." The husband realized that she was serious and asked her to pray for him. He was saved, and later gave up his position as photographer and became an Evangelist."

You see, the name of God meant something to this fine, Christian wife. She didn't like to hear God's name used irrelevantly. His name was hallowed to her. And because she took a strong stand for the name of God, her husband came to know Christ.

Let this story serve as a challenge to all Christian women. Let us firmly resolve to take a firm stand for whatever is right. This is our duty as Missionary women.

Reading: *(Mission Lesson)*
The Influence of a Christian Woman In The Church

Edith Deen, *"All The Women of the Bible"* *(Referenced)*

"The earliest examples of Women's Ministry in the House of God, is found in Exodus 38:8.

After the Israelites had come out of Egypt, these women ministered at the door of the tent meeting place.

Qualities of a virtuous woman are given in Proverbs 31:10-31.

I Corinthians 14:34, 35, Women in the churches are admonished to keep silent. In this particular admonition, Paul was speaking to the Church at Corinth, a Greek city where for many generations, high-born women had lived in seclusion. Chloe was such a woman and may have very well been shocked by the loud-voiced railings of women of a lower station in life. Since all women were welcome in the new church, among these may have been many who had worshipped in pagan temples and had not yet sufficient experience to assume leadership in the church.

But how could Paul deny women an active part in the church when Christ had taught that men and women are equal before God? There is no evidence that Paul silenced the women. Lydia was his first convert in Europe, and his first sermon in Europe had been addressed to women on the banks of the river at Philippi. If these women had kept silent, the Christian gospel would not have spread as fast as it did over Europe.

Paul found Priscilla, too, a woman of great ability and intellect who became a leader in the Church at Corinth and later at Ephesus. He did not silence her. Nor did he silence Phebe, who was a deaconess at Cenchrea,

I Timothy 2:9, 10, Paul says to Timothy that women professing godliness should be judged by their good works, not by what they wear. Works, not words, were what counted with such women.

I Peter 3:5—Holy women are those who trust in God and whose adornment is a MEEK and QUIET SPIRIT.

In the 16th chapter of Romans, Paul listed 38 different believers as "helpers in Christ." Several women are in the number. Phebe was a servant of the church; also Priscilla and Mary.

Women have more influence and power than they will ever acknowledge. As Christians, They Can Move the World For Christ. Example; The Women of Samaria . . .

Influence is an intangible something which is nonetheless real. It is easier to observe than to define. It is divinely originated ENERGY PLANTED IN THE LIVES OF CHRISTIAN WOMEN.

Christian women can influence the Church for good or for the opposites. Priorities must be in place.

1. "Seek ye first the Kingdom of God . . ."
2. Prayer—We do not depend on our ability, but on God's. "His Spirit will strengthen our inward man," making us strong in the Lord. Satan dreads prayer. Prayer is the greatest power we have on earth.
3. Study God's Word—2 Timothy 2:15; "Study to show thyself approved unto God, a workman that needeth not to be ashamed, rightly dividing the word of God."
4. Share—Witness—Christian women are to share Christ's concern for the whole world.
5. Make Disciples-Missionary Challenge—"Go ye therefore, and teach all nations, baptizing them in the name of the Father, and of the Son, and of the Holy Ghost." Share.
6. Win Souls—God has said, "He that winneth souls is wise." Proverbs 11:30.

How Women Can Win Souls To Christ

I   Witness with your life; live that others may see Christ in you.
II. Witness with your mouth trusting the Holy Spirit to give Power to the Spoken word.
III Witness by tithes and offerings so that other may preach Christ and you will have fruit to abound to your account. Phil. 4:15.
IV Have *faith* in God—Care for people is perhaps the most dramatic way in which the Church witnesses to its faith. DO WE REALLY CARE?
V   Love—Agape Love—Christian love, such as Christ has for His own, is the only power that can save the world.

VI Compassion—Compassion is understanding plus action.
    For example: The Good Samaritan, Luke 10:30-35.
    —Priest—Passed on other side
    —Levite—Look and passed on
    —Samaritan—had compassion, bound his wounds, put him on his own beast and took him to an inn, on tomorrow he gave the host two pence, asking him to take care and upon return would repay him, if he spent more.

VII Obey God's Commandments: Let us be conscious at all times that "the Lord is in His Holy Temple—let all the earth keep silent before Him."
    How are we to guard our influence?
    Direction from God and His guidance in all endeavors.

VIII Don't Be A Stumbling Block—I Corinthians 8:9.
    "But take heed lest by any means this liberty of yours become a stumbling block to them that are weak."
    "Ye are the Salt of the Earth." Matt 5:13
    "Ye are the light of the World." Matt 5:14
    What does salt do? It makes food more enjoyable to taste. What does light do? It dispels darkness, providing for greater comfort and convenience.
    A Christian woman is as salt to help make life more enjoyable for all who are around her. As light, she is to help banish the burden and anguish of sin by the light of Holiness and the Grace of God.
    This is a tremendous responsibility, but a Christian woman is not left to do the job alone. Psalm 32:8 "I will instruct thee and teach thee in the way which thou shalt go and I will guide thee with mine eyes."

Salt acts to preserve, and the Christian woman must act to preserve the world from corruption and condemnation. As the "Light of the World, we are to witness to His faith through Personal Example and to manifest the light by his testimony and actions.

The Kingdom of Heaven, said Jesus is like leaven. As soon as each particle of dough is leavened it becomes the medium for transmitting the leaven to the adjoining particle. Even so every Christian woman who receives the leaven of the gospel becomes the medium for transmitting power to everyone she touches. Sharing Christ with others is the responsibility of every Christian Woman.

The supreme mission of the church is to keep every Christian in such a close and vital relationship with Christ that Christ may Think, Love, and Work through us. The Church will then be indeed the body of Christ, and the influence of the Christian woman in the Church will be used to lift up The Name of Jesus.

Women of the Bible—

Found in my mama's journals: SOME WOMEN OF THE BIBLE

These are women of the Bible whose lives and faith in God challenge the Christian women of today to great faith, and fidelity to God.

EVE: Mother of All Living   Genesis 3:20

Woman, like man, were created by God for a specific purpose. Eve has a definite role, therefore, in God's plan. Though she led the way for the fall of humankind, she was not accountable for it. Consequently, she could participate in God's redemption.

SARAH: Mother of Promise   Genesis 21:1-3

Sarah, the mother of Isaac, received proof positive that God fulfills His promises. From her life one can learn many profitable lessons; such as, the danger of becoming impatient with God, the futility of replacing God's plans with man's, the importance of unquestioning faith in God.

LOT'S WIFE: Woman of Rebellion   Luke 17:32

Rebellion is the root and essence of sin. Sin entered the universe when Lucifer rebelled against God. Sin entered the human race when Adam rebelled against God's word. Lots' wife, a sinful woman, exhibited a rebellious spirit in every facet of her life.

REBEKAH: Mother of Nations   Genesis 24:67; 25:23

A nation's overall morality is a reflection of the combined vices and virtues of its citizens. Righteous people produce righteous nations, and vice versa. Though God still has some dealings with nations, He is presently calling out a people unto Him (His church), from all nations.

JOCHEBED: Mother of Moses   Numbers 26:59

It has often been declared that behind every great man, stand a great woman. The life of Jochebed, the mother of Moses, certainly verifies this statement. Were if not for her undaunted faith in the true God, her son probably would not have been such a peerless leader.

MIRIAM: Woman of Service   Numbers 26:59

If Jochebed was the great woman who stood behind the great man Moses, Miriam was truly the great woman who stood beside him. As his sister, Miriam entire life was devoted service to Moses. It is seen, that all her activities centered around him.

RAHAB: Woman of Deliverance   Joshua 6:17

Because she was instrumental in the Israelites' possession of the Promised Land, Rahab has a piece in sacred history. Her deliverance from Jericho's destruction illustrated our salvation from sin's condemnation. Her being spared also resulted in her becoming an ancestor of Christ.

DEBORAH: Woman of Victory   Judges 4:4

Although God intended for men to assume the role of leadership in His work, situations sometime developed that men shirk their responsibilities. In such moments of crisis, God sometimes uses a woman to accomplish needed task.

RUTH: Woman of Fidelity   Ruth 1:14

Faithfulness is within the capability of every saint. Not everyone can preach, teach, sing, or serve in a specific office. But, everyone can be faithful to his church, the Lord, and God's cause. In Ruth's case faithfulness was generously rewarded. God shall do likewise by us.

HANNAH: Woman of Prayer   1 Samuel 1:9-10

Prayer has been termed, "the greatest force on earth." It is in fact the greatest source of power that is available to man. Even the weakest saint can resort to it and gain strength sufficient to meet any need. No Christian is strong enough, however, to neglect prayer.

BATHSHEBA: Mother of Kings   1 Kings 1:16-17

Jesus Christ, "the King of kings and Lord of lords," is destined to be the earth's Millennia Sovereign. Though He is now in exile in the "far country" of heaven, His claim to the throne cannot be refuted. Soon the Greater Son of great David shall exercise His rights, and exhibit His might.

JEZEBEL: Woman of Sin   II King 9:7

It is tragic for anyone to become steeped in sin. For a woman and a mother to do so is even worse because of the extensive consequences that are likely to result from it. Throughout the years women, and especially mothers, have been associated with high moral standards.

ESTHER: Woman of Courage   Esther 7:6

Christian courage is a most admirable quality. In view of Satan's dogged opposition to the Lord's work and His people, Christian courage is a sorely needed trait. The kind of fortitude that enables us to withstand trials—springs from strong convictions. These convictions are founded upon Godly principles. Hopefully Esther's examples encourage us accordingly.

ELISABETH: Mother of Credence   Luke 1:24, 25

The word credence suggests, "the fact of intellect assent without implying anything about ground of assent." This statement should describe pointedly our faith. True, genuine faith in God and His Word is unquestioning and unwavering. People of credence believe God, no matter the circumstances.

MARY: Mother of Christ   Luke 1:30-31

If strange things happened to Elizabeth, an even stranger incident was experienced by her cousin Mary. For some reason known only to the sovereign God, Mary was chosen to give birth to the long-promised Messiah. Though a difficult decision, Mary gave the consent of her will to God's.

THE SAMARITAN: Woman of Cleaning   John 4:7

Cleansing from sin was needed by all of Adam's descendant's. Though the degree of sinfulness may differ from one person to another, the fact of sinfulness remains unchanged. In view of mankind's need to hear the gospel, soul-winning by individuals, and churches, figures prominently in Gods plan of evangelism.

Trivia; Do you know who these women of the bible are?

Note: [A test that Mama put together to check biblical knowledge of women in the bible]. (Who is:)

1. The wife of Amram, and the mother of Miriam, Aaron, and Moses. Numbers 26:59
2. A maidservant in the house of Mary, mother of Mark, in Jerusalem who was the first to hear Peter knock at the gate after his miraculous escape from prison. Acts 12:13
3. A Hebrew prophetess to whom King Josiah sent his High Priest, Hilkiah to ask questions concerning the law book found in the temple. II Chronicles 34:22
4. As the second wife of Herod, she demanded, through her daughter, the head of John the Baptist, because he had denounced her marriage. Matthew 14:3-11
5. She and her sons knelt before Jesus, and she said, "Grant that these my two sons may sit, the one the right hand and the other on the left, in thy kingdom. Matthew 20:20-23-Matthew 27:56
6. When Jesus came into her country, she entreated Him to heal her afflicted daughter. Jesus healed the daughter without even seeing her. Mark 7:24-30
7. She is chosen to be wife of King Ahasuerus of Persia. Her service to her people gave rise to the Feast of Purim. Ester 9:22-29
8. A seller of purple dye, she lives at Philippi, but is a native of Thyatira in Asia Minor. She and all her household were baptized by Paul. Acts16:14-15
9. This woman and her husband withhold money for themselves that was dedicated to the common good. Upon Peter confronting her with her falsehood, she lies to him. Acts 5:1-11
10. They were responsible for providing Timothy with the proper training of trusting in the Lord during his early childhood. II Timothy 1:5
11. Sews for the needy at Joppa. When she dies suddenly, those she befriended send for Peter and show him garments she made. He prays fervently and raises her from the dead. Acts 9:36-41
12. Daughter of the king of the Zidonians, and worshipper of Baal, she becomes wife of King Ahab of Northern Israel. I King 16:28-31
13. Jesus cast seven demons out of this woman. She becomes one of his faithful followers, going with him all the way to the cross. Luke 8:2

14. Offered hospitality of her home to the Prophet Elisha. Turns over upper room to him. He tells her that she shall have a son in due time. II King 4:8-37
15. A woman representing the Philistines who were enemies of Samson, she betrays him for money. Learning that his strength was in his hair, she has it shaved off. Judges 16:2-31
16. A prophetess, Judge of Israel, and wife of Lapidoth, she becomes a woman of great power. With Barak she leads the people to victory. Judges 4:4
17. She was the wife of Abraham and she also lived one hundred and twenty-seven years. Genesis 23:1
18. Job's third daughter, whose name meant "born of antimony," an eye paint that was used as a beautifier by oriental women to make their eyes large and lustrous. She was born after her father's great trials, when his wealth, health and honor had been restored. Job 42:13-14
19. One of Solomon's many wives, who became the mother of King Rehoboam, last King of the united monarchy of David and Solomon, and first ruler of the southern Kingdom of Judah. I King 14:21
20. King Saul's eldest daughter, who had been promised to David for his prowess in slaying the Philistine Goliath. I Samuel 18:17
21. The wife of Amaziah, king of Judah, who brought back idols of the Edomites, and set them up for his gods. Her son was Uzziah, King of Judah. II Chronicles 26:3
22. Her name means; "deceitful." She is the only woman in the Bible of whom it is written that a javelin was thrust "through her belly." Numbers 25:15

Answers: *(Not in order):*

Sarah
Queen Ester
Midianite Woman (Cozbi)
Jochebed
Deborah
Delilah
Merab
Naamah
Jezebel
Shunammite
Jecoliah
Huldah
Keren-happuch
Herodias
Mother of Zebedee's Children (Salome)
The Syrophoenician (Greek) Woman
Mary Magdalene
Sapphira
Tabitha
Rhonda
Lydia
Eunice—Lois

Chapter 8

Essays

Essay—Mama Wrote It in 1968
The American Home—Our Greatest Heritage

The foundation of our whole life—physical, emotional, mental, and spiritual—are laid in the American home. The well-ordered and well-kept home based on love, mutual helpfulness, and intelligent cooperation is the greatest heritage and achievement of mankind.

The American home is the one place in all the world where hearts are sure of each other. It is the place where we tear off that mask of guarded and suspicious coldness which the world forces us to wear in self-defense.

By living and working together in the home, we acquire virtues, skills, and habits essential to the highest success in life. Sharing responsibilities in the home, one learns to think, to plan, and to cooperate with others in ways that will help build better schools, stronger churches, and finer communities.

Our forefathers struggled and sacrificed their lives to establish and to preserve the American home. The task was not easy, but they knew the importance of the home. They realized that the home is the first and the greatest institution of learning.

Yes, the home—trailer, cottage, or shack—is the backbone of our great society. It is in our homes that America has put her trust. Years of research and study reveal that the American home is our greatest heritage. The challenge is to every citizen to exalt, enrich and beautify your home. It is the foundation of your life and happiness; the first school of citizenship and democracy.

Think and visualize for one moment the thousands of homeless people throughout the universe today, and compare their lives with the average American. You will find that while we are secure in our homes, many nations are peopled with homeless citizens. These forsaken folk roam the streets day and night seeking shelter and rest any place they can get it. Often, they are sick, tired, and lonely, for to them there is no place called home.

Grace Crowell in her poem, "So Long as There Are Homes," shows that the American home has its roots in religious belief. As long as Americans believe in God and let Him guide and direct their homes, the American Home will remain our greatest heritage. In the words of the poet, let us always remember: "So long as there are homes which men turn at close of day; So long as there are homes where children are, where women stay; if love and loyalty and faith be found across these sills, a stricken nation can recover from its gravest ills. So long as there are homes where lamps are lit and prayers are said; Although people falter through the dark and nations grope; With God Himself back of these little homes, We sure have hope."

These are a few of my **Mama's**
STORIES,
PHILOSOPHIES,
WORDS of WISDOM,
HOPE THOUGHTS,
INSIGHTS TO GROW ON,
AND
REFLECTIONS ON THE WONDERS OF THE WORLD
Poems and Proverbs

Written by My Mama; Mrs. Louisteen Harris

Patricia L. Harris-Cook, Daughter

My Mama's Personal Journal

A living, growing book, with blank pages to plant ideas and nourish dreams: Dated 5/30/82;

- Read the Gospels and Acts four (4) times in 30 days.
- Put God's word first in your life and all the other things will get done.
- Don't be critical of other people. If someone tries to share negative things with you, pause and say, "Let's pray for the person."
- Surrender our will to God's will.
- There is no defeat in God.
- I Peter 5:7—"Casting all your care upon Him; for He careth for you."
- Proverbs 13:22 "... and the wealth of the sinner is laid up for the just."
- If a wise man contendeth with a foolish man, whether he rage or laugh, there is no rest." Proverbs 29:9.
- Service makes us Great. Matthew 20:20-28.
- God is the giver of good gifts.
- Keep your eyes on the giver, and not the gifts.
- The church is a hospital for sinners, and not a museum for saints.
- Man is no match for Satan. The only hope for man is to reach out to God.
- Faith is conviction that God told the truth.
- "Partial obedience—is disobedience" *Dr. C. Stanley*
- The Judge of the earth will do right.
- There are 32,000 promises in the Bible.
- "Make your scars into stars." *Robert Schuler*
- When praying say, "In the Name of Jesus," because of Calvary, deliverance will manifest.
- The secret of deliverance is instant obedience.
- Our thoughts are our talk. "I am what I think."
- Our attitudes are more important than circumstance.
- You believe and then see. Faith comes before sight.
- "Your attitude will determine your altitude.
- Moses learned that what you do is worthless unless God is in the Plan.
- God will provide the miracle to match every mountain.
- "Poor Taste"—To hit a person's Achilles' heel is considered poor taste. Achilles' heel: one's vulnerable spot.
- Brotherhood: "Honor all men. Love the brotherhood. Fear God. Honor the King." I Peter 2:17

The Gospel Alphabet
Composed by My Mama

A All have sinned and come short of the glory of God. Rom 3:23.
B Behold the Lamb of God, which taketh away the sin of the world. John 1:29.
C Come unto me, all ye that labor and are heavy laden, and I will give you rest. Matt.11:28.
D Draw nigh to God, and He will draw nigh to you. James 4:8.
E Even so it is not the will of your Father which is in Heaven that one of these little ones should perish. Matthew 18:14.
F For by grace are ye saved through faith; and that not of yourselves: it is the gift of God: Eph 2:8.
G God is our refuge and strength, a very present help in trouble. Psalms 46:1.
H Him that cometh to me I will in no wise cast out. John 6:37.
I I am the way, the truth, and the life: no man cometh unto the Father, but by me. John 14:6.
J Jesus answered and said unto them, This is the work of God, that ye believe on him whom he hast sent. John 6:29.
K Knock, and it shall be opened unto you. Matthew 7:7.
L Look unto me, and be ye saved, all the ends of the earth. Isa. 45:22.
M My grace is sufficient for thee. 2 Cor. 12:9.
N Now is the day of salvation. 2 Cor. 6:2.
O Our Passover also hath been sacrificed, even Christ. I Cor.5:7
P Peace I leave with you: My peace I give unto you. John 14:27.
Q Quicken me according to Thy Word. Psalms. 119:154.
R Redeemed us from the curse of the law. Gal. 3:13.
S Suffer little children to come unto Me, and forbid them not: for of such is the kingdom of God. Luke 18:16.
T The blood of Jesus Christ his Son cleanseth us from all sin. I John 1:7.
U Unto you that fear my name shall the Sun of righteousness arise with healing in his wings . . . Mal. 4:2.
V Verily, verily, I say unto you, he that believeth on Me hath everlasting life. John 6:47.
W Who his own self bare our sins in his own body on the tree. I Peter 2:24.
X (Except) a man be born again, he cannot see the Kingdom of God. John 3:3
Y Ye must be born again. John 3:7.
Z Zealous of good works. Titus 2:14.

Patricia L. Harris-Cook, Daughter

Mama's Favorite
Alphabetical Bible Verses

A—Ask and it shall be given you; seek, and you shall find; knock, and it shall be opened unto you. Matthew 7:7.

B—Be not overcome of evil, but overcome evil with good. Romans 12:21.

C—Come unto me, all ye that labor, and are heavy laden, and I will give you rest. Matthew 11:28.

D—Deliver me, O Lord, from the evil man: preserve me from the violent man; Which imagine mischiefs in their heart; continually are they gathered together for war. Psalms 140: 1, 2.

E—Enter into his gates with Thanksgiving, and into his courts with praise: be thankful unto him, and bless his name. Psalms 100:4.

F—Fret not thyself because of evil-doers, neither be thou envious against the workers of iniquity. Psalms 37:1.

G—Grudge not one against another, brethren, lest ye be condemned: behold the judge standeth before the door. James 5:9.

H—Having therefore these promises dearly beloved, let us cleanse ourselves from all filthiness of the flesh and spirit, perfecting holiness in the fear of God. II Cor. 7:11.

I—I can do all things through Christ which strengtheneth me. Philippians 4:13.

J—Judge not, that ye be not judged. Matthew 7:1.

K—Keep thy foot when thou goest to the house of God, and be more ready to hear than to give sacrifice of fools: for they consider not that they do evil. Ecclesiastes 5:1.

L—Let not your heart be troubled: ye believe in God, believe also in me. John 14:1.

M—My help cometh from the Lord, which made heaven and earth. Psalms 121:2.

N—Now faith is the substance of things hoped for, the evidence of things not seen. Hebrews 11:1

O—Open rebuke is better than secret love. Proverbs 27:5.

—One Lord, one faith, and one baptism. One God and Father of all, who is above all, and through all, and in you all. Eph. 4:5, 6.

P—Preserve me, O God: for in thee do I put my trust. Psalms 16:1.

Q—Quench not the Spirit. I Thessalonians 5:19

—Quenched the violence of fire escaped the edge of the sword, out of weakness were make strong, waxed valiant in fight, turned to flight the armies of the aliens. Heb. 11:34.

—Quicken me after the loving-kindness; so shall I keep the testimony of the mouth. Psalms 119:88.

R—Rejoice evermore. I Thessalonians 5:16.

S—See that none render evil for evil unto any man; but ever follow that which is good both among yourselves and to all. I Thessalonians 5:15.

T—The Lord is my shepherd; I shall not want. Psalms 23:1.

U—Unto thee, O Lord, do I lift up my soul. Psalms 25:1.

V—Verily, verily I say unto you, He that entereth not by the door into the sheepfold, but climbeth up some other way, the same is a thief and a robber. St. John 10:1.

—Verily I say unto you, wheresoever this gospel shall be preached in the whole world, there shall also this, that this woman hath done, be told for a memorial of her. Matthew 26:13.

W—Watch and pray that ye enter not into temptation: the spirit indeed is willing, but the flesh is weak. Matthew 26:41.

X—(No verse)

Y—Ye are the light of the world. A city that is set on a hill cannot be hid. Matthew 5:14.

—Ye did run well; who did hinder you that ye should not obey the truth. Galatians 5:7.

Z—Zedekiah was one and twenty years old when he began to reign, and he reigned eleven years in Jerusalem. And his mother's name was Hamutal the daughter of Jeremiah of Libnah. Jeremiah 52:1.

* * *

Psalms—Insights To Grow On

- Blessed is the man that walketh not in the counsel of the ungodly, nor standeth in the way of sinners, nor sitteth in the seat of the scornful. Psalms 1:1.

- Create in me a clean heart, O God; and renew a right spirit within me. Psalms 51:10.

- Depart from evil, and do good; and dwell for evermore. Psalms 37:27.

- Delight thyself also in the Lord; and he shall give thee the desires of thine heart. Psalms 37:4.

- "Tragedy never leaves you where it found you—you will change either for the 'good' or 'bad'." R. Schuler

Patricia L. Harris-Cook, Daughter

Hope Thoughts

FOR WITH THE HEART . . . Romans 10:10

It is always with the heart that man believes—and with his mouth he makes his confession.

As you read some of the "in Christ," "in Him," "in Whom"; etc. scriptures . . . they won't seem real to you. It may not seem as though you really have what these scriptures say you have in Him. But if you will begin to confess with your mouth, because you do believe God's Word in your heart, "This is mine. This is who I am. This is what I have," then, it will become reality to you. It is already real in the spirit realm. But we want it to become real in the physical realm where we live in the flesh.

1. Underline the Scripture.
2. Write it down.
3. Meditate on it.
4. Make a confession of it.
5. Begin to say it with your mouth.

The Great Confession—Romans 10:9, 10

Romans 10:9 That if thou shalt confess with thy mouth the Lord Jesus, and shalt believe in thine heart that God raised him from the dead, thou shalt be saved.

Romans 10:10: For with the heart man believeth unto righteousness; and with the mouth confession is made unto salvation.

Confession: I believe in my heart Jesus Christ is the Son of God. I believe He was raised from the dead for my justification. I confess Him as my Lord and Savior. Jesus is my Lord. He is dominating my life. He is guiding me. He is leading me.

When you believe a thing in your heart and confess it with your mouth, then, it becomes real to you.

Mama's Proverbial Notes: Dated; 6/25/83
Proverbs: God's Kind of Woman

o   Pray that God will fill us with His spirit daily.
    She is saved. She is filled with the Holy Spirit.
o   Sin and unforgiveness will block our understanding of the world.
    I John 1:9—"If we confess our sins, he is faithful and just to forgive us our sins, and to cleanse us from all unrighteousness."
    Proverbs 28:13—"He that covereth his sins shall not prosper: but whoso confesseth and forsaketh them shall have mercy."
o   Father with godly sorry, Please forgive me of the sin(s) of _____.
o   Father give me Godly sorrow for iniquity in my heart.
o   Help me to admit wrongs done—even wrongs done to children for they too are children of God.
o   Teach me to show more affection to my husband & my children.
    Mark 11:25, 26—"And when ye stand praying, forgive, if ye have ought against any: that your Father also which is in heaven may forgive you your trespasses."
o   But if ye do not forgive, neither will your Father which is in heaven forgive your trespasses.
o   "Except the Lord build the house, they labor in vain that build it: except the Lord keep the city, the watchman waketh but in vain." Psalms 127:1
o   Whatever is truly yours will come back to you if you let it go.

* * *

Writing Notations; by My Mama on:
10/06/84:
"Begin at the bottom—But believe in the top." Dr. R. Schuler

08/26/85:
God promised, "You shall eat the riches of the Gentiles. Isa. 61:6.

"God is the sum total of all, the unknown." Dr. R. Schuler

Love Words—In Appreciation
For acts of kindness received from well-wishers during grief.

Perhaps you prayed a prayer or come to call;
Perhaps you sent beautiful flowers, if so we saw them all.
Perhaps you sent or spoke kind words as any friend would say.
Perhaps you were not there at all, but just thought of us that day.
Perhaps you prepared some tasty dish or maybe furnished a car;
Whatever you did to console the heart by word or deed or touch;
Whatever was the kindly part,
We thank you, oh, so much.

The Family

Patricia L. Harris-Cook, Daughter

Stories, Lovewords, Hopethoughts, Philosophies, Words Of Wisdom, Insights To Grow On And Reflections Of The Wonder Of The World
By Louisteen Harris
Mama's Favorite

YOUR POWER TO SAY "NO"

"Happiness is to not have to explain anything to anyone. So notice how much unhappiness is included in explaining yourself to other people. The apologetic attitude has gone so far in some faces and manners that you see little else of their owners. How pathetic and how useless.

Timid explanations and apologies are based in fear. And fear is based in an individual's false self, the self made up of all his delusory beliefs about himself. This invented identity continues to control a life only because the individual carelessly says 'yes' to it all day long. But with less yeses the "no" will grow and the compulsive need to explain falls away.

When you don't want to say yes you don't have to say yes! Your "no" is your sacred right. No other human being on earth has power over it. It belongs to you alone." *(V. Howard)*

* * *

Looking Out For Number One!

"Get it out of your head that you're an Elastic man. You can't stretch in every direction at once. The result of trying to spread yourself too thin among friends is, quite naturally a reduction in the quality of your friendships. The easiest thing in the world is to make commitments; the hardest is to keep them. Don't leave the word, "yes," lying around on the tip of your tongue; Put it away somewhere for safekeeping, to be used for special occasions. You're far better off, in the long run, if you learn to say "NO" politely and pleasantly, but immediately and firmly."

"Over-volunteering is even worse than over-committing oneself. In a desire to make or keep friends, many people develop the dangerous habit of trying to solve everyone's problems. If you make this mistake, all too often the result is that somehow you end up being the 'bad guy,' while those who didn't offer to lift a finger get off scot-free. Back to the You-Won't-Get-Credit-For-It Theory: if you go overboard trying to be good guy (by becoming too involved in others' problems), you run a high risk of being tagged a 'bad guy' in the end. It can be a very frustrating experience, to say the least." *(R. J. Ringer)*

Murphy's Law

Nothing is as easy as it looks. {Everything takes longer than you think; except}. And if anything can go wrong—it will. At the worst possible moment!

"And ye shall eat in plenty, and be satisfied and praise the name of the Lord your God, that hath dealt wondrously with you: and my people shall never be ashamed." Joel 2:26

"And it shall come to pass afterward, that I will pour out my spirit upon all flesh; and your sons and your daughters shall prophesy, your old men shall dream dreams, your young men shall see visions." Joel 2:28

"And also upon the servants and upon the handmaids in those days will I pour out my spirit." Joel 2:29

Quote by My Mama: "If we obey God and make Him our Source, give tithes of all, we will be healed of all diseases and blessed spiritually, financially, etc. Withholding from God prevents our miracles. We cannot live without God as our Source."

How To Keep Going . . .
When The Going Gets Tough

Why Do We Face Rough Times?
- Sometimes we cause them ourselves
- Satan
- God allows them.

How Do We Respond to Rough Times?
- Blame God or someone else {Rebel to God}
- Run . . . Get out of the circumstance.
- Head for the pill or the bottle.
- Commit suicide. {This is never the answer}.

God's Way To Keep Going:
- Go in the strength of God. Isaiah 50:9-11, 24-26, 31.
- Commune with God.
- Quietness Before Him
- Trusting in Him.
- Expecting from Him

The House Of God

"And let them make me a sanctuary; that I may dwell among them." Exodus 25:8

"No weapon that is formed against thee shall prosper; and every tongue that shall rise against thee in judgment thou shalt condemn. This is the heritage of the servants of the Lord, and their righteousness is of me, saith the Lord." Isaiah 54:17.

O GIVE THANKS

O Give thanks unto the Lord; for he is good;
for his mercy endureth for ever.
O Give thanks unto the God of gods;
for his mercy endureth for ever.
O Give thanks to the Lord of lords;
for his mercy endureth for ever.
To him who alone doeth great wonders;
for his mercy endureth for ever.
To him that by wisdom made the heavens;
for his mercy endureth for ever. Psalms 136:1-5.

Chapter 9

Term Papers, Theme Papers . . .

You Name It . . . "My Mama Wrote It"

Hercules

The most celebrated of all the Greek heroes was the mighty and great hearted Hercules. In Greek the word is Heractes. He was the son of the Greek god, Zeus, and his mother, Alcmene, was a princess.

Hera, wife of Zeus, was jealous of the mortal Alcmene, and she hated Hercules from infancy.

Hercules is the latinized form of the most famous Greek legendary hero. Its probable meaning, "glorious gift of Hero," shows that he could not have been an original god because no Greek god has a name compounded from another deity. Underneath his very complicated mythology, there is probably concealed a real man, perhaps a chieftain vassal of the kingdom of Argos.

His legend gives him divine parentage. Zeus, wanting a powerful son among both gods and men, begot him.

Hera used trickery to deny the mighty Hercules from inheriting the throne and becoming king. This was accomplished by causing the son of Sthenulus to be born prematurely so that Hercules would not be the first born son as nature had planned. As a result, Eurystheus was the first born, and as was the custom, he became the king.

Eurystheus was a sick and feeble king. In spite of this he was still cruel to Hercules. He forced Hercules to take service under him. Hercules was assigned many, evil tasks throughout his lifetime; however he was successful in accomplishing each and every one of them.

As mentioned earlier in this writing, Hera hated Hercules. When Hercules married Megara a Theban princess, Hera made him become insane, and he burned his house, killing his wife and children. Upon recovering his sanity, Hercules sought help from the oracle of Delphi. The oracle told him he must serve his cousin, Eurystheus, King of Argos, for twelve years. He was compelled to perform the great task known as the twelve labors. To atone for his terrible sin, Hercules set out to perform these labors. They were as follows:

First, he killed the Nemean Lion by thrusting his arm down its throat thereby strangling him. With difficulty, he removed the tough skin and wore it as an armor.

The second labor was to kill Hydra, a serpent with nine venomous heads. The Hydra grew two heads that replaced every head that Hercules cut off. He burned off eight of the heads, but the ninth head was immortal. He buried the ninth head under a stone. Hercules dipped his arrows in the Hydra's venom to make them fatally poisonous. As soon as Hercules chopped off a head, Iolaus burned the neck with fire. The middle head could not be burned.

In the third labor, Hercules captured the Ceryneian stag.

The fourth labor consisted of killing a wild boar in the Arcadian mountains. This animal had golden horns and brass-like hooves.

As the fifth labor, Hercules drove away a huge flock of Stymphalian birds that lived near Lake Stymphalus in Arcadia. This great flock of destructive birds lived and thrived on human flesh.

The sixth labor was to clean the stables of King Augeas of Elis in one day. The dirty stables held a herd of three thousand oxen and had not been cleaned for thirty years. Hercules turned two large rivers through the stables and cleaned them in a single day.

For the seventh labor, Hercules went to Crete and caught the savage bull of Minos, the Cretan bull.

The eighth labor was to capture the man-eating mares of King Diomedes of Trace. Hercules killed Diomedes and fed his flesh to the horses. Upon eating the flesh of Diomedes, the horses became gentle.

The ninth labor was to obtain the girdle of the Amazon queen, Hippolyta. According to ancient Greek tradition, the Amazons were a race of war-like women who made slaves of the men they captured. They lived along the banks of the River Thermodon in Asia Minor. The largest city they built was Ephesus. There they built many magnificent temples for the worship of Ares and Artemis. Hercules was said to have great strength, courage, and good nature but also to be easily angered.

During his tenth labor, Hercules was required to travel to Erytheia, in order to capture the oxen of Geryon. The oxen fell victim to an arrow which had been dipped in venomous blood. During his tenth labor, Hercules in addition to capturing the oxen of Geryon, also split a mountain into.

The eleventh labor was to carry the apples of the Hesperides to Eurystheus. These golden apples were guarded by four sister nymphs called the Hesperides. Their father, Atlas, had to hold up the heaven; but Hercules did this for him while Atlas secured the apples.

The twelfth labor, Hercules had to show Cerberus, the watch dog of the Lower World, to Eurystheus. He succeeded in seizing the monster and carrying it to Eurystheus. After capturing Cerberus, the many headed dog who guarded the gates of the underworld, the King was so terrified that Hercules had to return the monster to Hades.

The last three labors were ways of winning immortality, because Geryon and Cerberus represent Death, and the apples were the fruit of the "Tree of Life."

Hercules was now a free man, but he still performed several outstanding tasks. Some of them are as follows:

1. He freed Prometheus from a chained rock. Prometheus was an immortal member of a group of giant gods called Titans. He and his brother, Epimetheus, were assigned by the gods to give the animals the powers they needed. Epimetheus worked hard at this task, but when it was man's turn, there was no gift left.
Prometheus took pity on the helplessness of primitive man. He stole fire from the gods and gave it to man. Zeus was so angered that he caused Prometheus to be chained to Mount Caucasus. A vulture came every day to tear at his liver, and every night the liver grew again. Prometheus suffered for thousands of years. At last, Hercules killed the vulture and set Prometheus free.

2. He accompanied the Argonauts in their search for the Golden Fleece. In Greek mythology, Golden Fleece, was the golden wool of the sacred ram Chrysomallus. The fleece hung from a tree in a forest near the Black Sea, and a fierce dragon who never slept guarded it.
Argonauts were a group of heroes in Greek mythology. They sailed with their leader, Jason, on the ship Argo. They had many adventures on the way

to Colchis, including their successful passage through the Clashing Rocks which were powerful enough to crush a ship.

In Colchis, the king's daughter Medea, fell in love with Jason and helped him perform the tasks which her father assigned him. She then helped Jason and the Argonauts capture the Golden Fleece, and sailed back to Greece with them.

They had to go a long way around to get back to Greece. They met many dangers on the way, but the Argonauts and the courageous Hercules returned home with the Golden Fleece.

3. Hercules, in a temper tantrum, killed his friend, Iphitus. For this crime he had to serve Queen Omphale of Lydia for three years.

4. He married Deinira. She gave him a shirt which had been dipped in the blood of the centaur Nessus, whom Hercules slew. Hercules put the shirt on and it clung to him so snugly that he tore pieces of his own flesh off in his desperate attempt to tear off this horrible garment.

In his agony, he built a pyre on Mount Oeta and threw himself upon it. He was burned to death, whereupon, he was borne away to heaven in a thick cloud and became a god.

5. He brought Alcestis back to life. Alcestis, the wife of Admetus, the mythical king of Thessaly, volunteered to die in her husband's place. Admetus aroused the anger of Diana, and she ruled that he would die young. Apollo arranged that if someone would die for Admetus, his life would be saved. Alcestis bravely took his place as his friends and relatives had refused to save him. As Admetus began to mourn, Hercules came to the palace. Upon hearing of Alcestis's fate, he went to the grave, outwrestled Death, and brought her back alive.

6. He married Hebe. Hebe was a goddess in Greek mythology, daughter of Jupiter and Hera. She filled the cups of the gods with nectar. On day she tripped and fell. Jupiter dismissed her, and in the shape of an eagle he went to earth to seize Ganymede to serve the gods.

Hebe was a goddess of youth. She had power to make old people young again. Hercules married her after he was made a god. Hebe ended the long quarrel between Hercules and his stepmother, Hera.

Hera, the divine wife of Zeus, hated Hercules. While he was still in the cradle, she sent two serpents to kill him. Instead of the serpents destroying

Hercules, he strangled them. This really made Hera angry. She tried in every way to destroy him, but each time he was the victor.

In early childhood, Hercules spent many hours daily developing his muscles by properly exercising them. It paid big dividends for him. Not only did he conquer all his tasks, he also conquered death.

He was educated by Chiron, the wise Centaur. Hercules was worshipped by both the Greeks and the Romans as a god.

7. He waged a war against the kingdom of Orchonenus in Boetia and married Megara one of its royal princess; however he killed her in a fit of madness caused by that wicked Hera.

When Hercules was a young man, two beautiful maidens appear in his life. One was Arete (virtue); the other Kakia (vice). Kakia offered him ease, pleasure, and riches if he would follow her. Arete offered him only glory for a life long struggle against evil. Hercules chose to be guided by Arete.

At the end of his life Hercules won immortality. He was traveling with Deinira, his wife, and he allowed a centaur, named Nessus to carry her across a flooded stream. Nessus was rude to her, and Hercules shot him with a poisoned arrow. As Nessus died, he told Deianira to save his blood to use as a love charm. When Hercules later fell in love with Ione, a woman he captured, Deianira dipped a robe in the blood and sent it to him. When he put it on, the poison ate away his flesh. In agony, he begged his friends to place him on a funeral pyre, and light it. After his body had been burned up, he was taken up into Olympus and welcomed as one of the gods.

Hercules heroic strength has inspired many works of art. The finest representation in sculpture is the so called Farnese Hercules in the National Museum at Naples. It is a copy of an early work by the ancient sculptor, Lysippus.

The writer was deeply interested in Hercules. The story of his life and his life after death, although legendary, paints a vivid picture of man in his eternal quest of love, honor, and happiness. Tales of this nature tend to encourage people to "fight" constantly to improve their earthly role.

Of special interest to me was how every one told of Hercules a man of great strength, courage and good nature; however he had a weakness. He was easily angered. This shows the imperfection of mankind. Regardless to how good, how strong, and how brave one might be, he generally has a weak spot. The beauty of this comparison reveals too that each of us has a "good side;" therefore it is wise to learn to develop the very best that is in us.

Bibliography

1. *The World Book Encyclopedia*, Volume 8, Field Enterprises Educational Corporation, Chicago, Illinois.
2. *Britannica Junior* Encyclopedia, Volume 7, Encyclopedia Britannica, Inc., Chicago, Illinois.
3. *Italy*, Kish, George, Nelson Doubleday, Inc., Garden City, New York.
4. *The Best of the World's Classics*, Volume II, Rome, by Lodge, Henry Cobot and Halsey Francis, Funk & Wagnall's Company, New York.

The Picturesque Account of Thomas Jefferson

I   Early Childhood
    A. Family Background
    B. Education
II Late Childhood
    A. College Training
    B. Cultural Growth
III Manhood
    A. Courtship
    B. Marriage
    C. Procreation
IV Occupations
    A. Lawyer
    B. National Statesman
    C. Writer
    D. Governor
    E. Minister to France
    F. Congressman
    G. Secretary of State
    H. Vice-President
    I. President
V   Senior Years
    A. Accomplishments
    B. Religion
    C. Death

The Picturesque Account of Thomas Jefferson

Thomas Jefferson, the eldest son of Peter Jefferson and Jane Randolph, was born on April 13, 1743, at Shadwell, the family farm in Albemarle County, Virginia. "The Shadwell homestead was named from his mother," who first saw the light in a London parish of that name." [1]

"Young Thomas had a good start. His father was a land surveyor, only a few years before George Washington undertook the same business. The owner of Shadwell farm was a Hercules in strength and stature. He singly performed feats which taxed the powers of three strong men. But he was also a man of much intelligence, shrewd sense, and force of character. County honors naturally gravitated to such a one. In due time, the Shadwell farmer became Justice of the Peace, Colonel at Albemarle County and Representative in the House of Burgesses." [2]

"Jane Randolph, who came from the old Virginia stock, could never have regretted the choice of her youth, although her early married life must have involved many privations and hardships." [3]

"Thomas grew up with the normal interest of a country boy—hunting, fishing, horseback riding, and canoeing. His father taught him to read and

---

[1] De Vries, Julian, *Lives of the Presidents* (Cleveland, Ohio: World Publishing Co., 1944) P.33.

[2] Ibid. P.33

[3] Ibid. P.33.

write and to keep the farm accounts. The youth also learned to play the violin and to love music." [4]

Little Thomas was the first son, but he had two big sisters. His parents eventually became the "heirs" of six girls and five boys.

The "death angel" carried Peter Jefferson to Heaven when Thomas was merely fourteen years old. As the oldest son, he became his own master and head of the family. "He inherited Shadwell with its thirty (30) slaves and more than 2,500 acres of land." [5]

Thomas left the management of the home estate to his guardian, John Harvey, and entered the school of the Reverend James Maury, whose school was regarded as the best in Virginia. He studied at this parsonage for two years.

In 1760, Thomas enrolled in the college of William and Mary located in Williamsburg, Virginia. He graduated in 1762.

At William and Mary, young Jefferson met William Small and Judge George Wythe. These men had a great influence on Thomas. Many of his basic ideas about God, the universe, his county, et cetera were molded and shaped as a result of his studies and the companionship of these cultured men.

Upon completing his college work, Jefferson studied law with Judge Wythe.

Throughout Thomas Jefferson's school career, his teachers were aware of his superb intelligence. Not only was he a good student, he was an expert violinist. As legend goes, Jefferson won his fair bride because of his love for music. "Two rival suitors came to call one day, but left without a word when they saw the couple playing a duet on the harpsichord and violin." [6]

"The first romance of his life came to him before he was nineteen years old. The charms of Belinda or Rebecca Burwell proved powerful enough to

---

[4] "Thomas Jefferson," *World Book Encyclopedia* (1962), X, P.58.
[5] Ibid. P.58
[6] Ibid. P. 60.

win the thoughts of the devoted student from his book but she was married soon afterward, and Jefferson's young romance was shattered. He believed his heart would never rally from that blow." [7]

In 1772, Jefferson married Martha Wayles Skelton, a young widow and the daughter of a prominent lawyer, John Wayles. The bride was a woman of grace and charm. She was tall with auburn hair, and a slight fragile figure. Martha was gifted in singing and playing the harpsichord.

The Jefferson's settled at Monticello. They had six children, a boy and five girls. Only two children lived to maturity. "The eldest who bore the beloved name of Martha, survived him, but the others seemed to have inherited their mother's fragile constitution. Four died in infancy. Mary, the fourth child, reach young womanhood." [8]

Mrs. Jefferson died on September 6, 1782, only ten years after marrying Thomas Jefferson. The shock literally drove Jefferson insane. He refused to visit or write his friends. A few months later he told a friend, "A single event wiped out all my plans and left me a blank which I had not the spirit to fill up." His daughter, Martha, wrote many years later: ". . . the violence of his emotion . . . to this day I dare not describe to myself." [9]

Mr. Jefferson was admitted to the bar in 1767. He was a successful lawyer until public service began taking all his time. Dividing his time with law practice and building his own home, Monticello, proved to be a huge chore.

Jefferson became a statesman in 1769 and served in this capacity until 1775. He was not a gifted speaker, but he excelled as a writer of a variety of laws and resolutions.

The Declaration of Independence is probably the most renown of Jefferson's writings. This famous document states; "that men are by nature endowed with certain inalienable rights; that governments are instituted to preserve

---

[7] De Vries, *op. cit.* P.34.
[8] *Ibid.* P. 39.
[9] *Ibid.* P. 62

these rights; that governments derive their just powers from the consent of the governed; that the governed may alter or abolish their government if it proves destructive of the ends for which it was established . . ." [10]

"The declaration was received with wild rejoicing, "as though," said Samuel Adams, "it was a decree promulgated from heaven." [11]

Other Writings included:

1. *Notes on Virginia.* In this book, Jefferson includes a vast amount of information on Virginia and a few of his personal beliefs and ideals.
2. *Manual of Parliamentary Practice.* The manual was written during the time Jefferson was Vice-President. It was used to aid deliberations in presiding over the Senate. It proved valuable and is still used widely.
3. *"Letter To Thomas Jefferson Randolph."* This letter was written near the end of Jefferson's second term as President. It was written to his grandson, Thomas Jefferson Randolph, a student in college. The lad was given helpful advise in the realm of getting along with his peers.
4. *"Portrait from Memory."* "In a letter written from Monticello when he was seventy, Jefferson set down his impressions of a great American who had died fourteen years before. The portrait is an honest one; instead of a flawless legend. It presents a human being, with human virtues and failings." [12]

"The Virginia Assembly elected Jefferson governor for one year terms in 1779 and 1780. During his administration, the state suffered severely from the effects of the Revolutionary War. Jefferson had stripped Virginia of its defenses in order to aid the American Army. James Monroe was called upon to recruit Virginians for military service." [13]

---

[10] Homer Hockett, *Political and Social Growth of the American People* (New York: The Macmillan Company, 1940), P. 201
[11] *Ibid.* P. 202
[12] Mark Schorer, Arno Jewett, Walter Havighurst, and Allen Kirschner, *American Literature* (Boston: Houghton Mifflin Co., 1968), P. 178
[13] "Thomas Jefferson," *World Book Encyclopedia* (1962 ed.), *X*, P. 62.

In 1781, British troops invaded Virginia. Jefferson barely escaped capture. Although reelected by the legislature, Governor Jefferson declined the post because of his dislike for war and returned to his home, Monticello. Here he planned to live a simple, quiet life, but fate took his wife and left him grief stricken.

In 1783, his countrymen elected him to Congress. He accepted the position because he needed something to help erase the burden of his personal tragedy. Some of his accomplishments were as follows:
Served as chairman of several committees, devised a decimal system of currency, piloted through Congress the Treaty of Paris, worked on the Ordinance of 1784, and the Land Ordinance of 1785.

Little did Jefferson know that a greater honor and a larger sphere of action were awaiting him. In 1784, Congress appointed him to a new post, Minister to France. He was to receive $9,000.00 a year for this appointment. "But despite all that was novel, interesting, and delightful in that new life in Paris, it had its drawbacks. Jefferson could not speak French, and at his age it is not easy to learn a new language. Then his salary was inadequate as his position of foreign minister involved large expenses. The climate did not suit him as he was accustomed to a clear, warmer atmosphere." [14]

"But he saw all that was most brilliant, distinguished and charming in French society. The most illustrious people met under the American's roof. Despite his broken French, they liked him immensely." [15]

The picture Jefferson saw of the French people during his five year tenure was described by him as unutterable misery, ignorance, and oppression. He believed that of the twenty million inhabitants in France, nineteen million were suffering for food, clothing, and shelter. His residence in France only strengthened his loyalty and devotion to America.

The French Revolution occurred while Jefferson was in Paris. Although he sympathized with the revolution, he tried to steer clear of French politics.

---

[14] De Vries, *op. cit.* P. 44.
[15] *Ibid.* P. 44.

"Jefferson had taken his daughter, Martha, to France with him, and Mary joined them in 1787. Both girls attended a convent school in Paris. Jefferson traveled wide in Europe. He broadened his knowledge of many subjects, especially architecture and farming. He applied for a leave in 1789 and sailed for home in October. He wanted to settle his affairs in America and to take his daughters back home. Jefferson expected to return to represent the United States in France." [16]

Upon his arrival in the United States, a letter from George Washington awaited him, asking Jefferson to be Secretary of State in the newly formed government. After much hesitation, he accepted the position.

Alexander Hamilton was Secretary of the Treasury. Jefferson and Hamilton had many sharp, bitter differences of opinions. Hamilton, although of humble origin, had very little faith in the common people. He wanted the government to be governed by the aristocratic, rich people. Jefferson, a firm believer of the people, disagreed with him. A bitter feud developed between these two great men. This feud led to the establishing of the first political parties. The Federalist accepted Hamilton's principles. Jefferson was the leader of the Democratic-Republicans which in later years became known as the Democratic party.

Disgusted and tired, Mr. Jefferson resigned as Secretary of State on January 1, 1794. "But the nation could not leave him alone to experiment with his crops, and delight his soul with architecture and read his books, and talk in the pleasant evenings with his guests at Monticello. In 1796, he was elected Vice-President of the United States." [17]

John Adams, the President, and Thomas Jefferson, the Vice-President, did not see eye-to-eye on any legislation. Relations between the two men grew more and more strained daily until the men completely broke their relationship in 1800.

Jefferson presided over the Senate skillfully. He wrote a famous manual, "Manual of Parliamentary Skills," to aid him in this capacity.

---

[16] "Jefferson.", *op. cit.* P. 63
[17] De Vries, *op. cit.* P. 48.

The Federalist passed the Alien and Sedition Acts. These acts deprived the Democratic-Republicans of freedom of speech and of the press. Jefferson led the attack against them. He prepared a series of resolutions, the Kentucky Resolutions. James Madison prepared the Virginia Resolutions. These resolutions set forth the "compact" theory of the Nation and gave the states the right to judge when this compact had been broken.

A new era was dawning in America. The Republican party had its birth. Thomas Jefferson was their ideal. In 1801, "the party of the people" made him third President of the United States.

"His entrance upon office formed an era of great changes in the administration. The inaugurals of our first two Presidents were full of stately ceremonials and elaborate etiquette . . . Everybody knows how Jefferson, true to his Democratic convictions, abolished all these. The third President of the United States rode into Washington on March 4, 1801, without guard or servant, dismounted, and hitched the horse's bridle to the fence with his own hands." [18]

"The most important event by far of Jefferson's first term was the purchase in 1803 of the Province of Louisiana, which spread its broad plains westward from the Mississippi River to the Rocky Mountains." [19]

"Fifteen million dollars and a stroke of a pen had nearly doubled the nation's size. In a message to Congress, the President justified the Louisiana Purchase: "The fertility of the country, its climate, and extent." Jefferson wrote, "promise in due season important aids to our Treasury, an ample provision for our posterity, and a wide spread for the blessing of freedom and equal laws." [20]

"The bargain was a great one for America. It not only precluded all possibility of a foreign power getting a footing on the lower Mississippi it also secured forever the control of the great river and added to the United States a vast, fertile domain of unknown bounds. As afterward ascertained, Louisiana contained 1,171,931 square miles—more than all the original thirteen states combined." [21]

---

[18] *Ibid*. P. 50.
[19] Hockett, *op. cit*. P. 377.
[20] Schorer, *op. cit*. P. 189.
[21] Henry Elson, *History of the United States* (New York: Macmillan, 1945), P. 362.

In 1804, Jefferson defeated the Federalist, Charles C. Pinckney, and began his second term as President of the United States. "Jefferson's second term, began as he later put it, "without a cloud on the horizon," but a storm soon began to gather." [22]

The trial of Aaron Burr for conspiracy, the passing of the unpopular Embargo Act, and the English outrages on American shipping in American waters made Jefferson's term a most miserable fulfillment.

Perhaps the happiest man in all America was Thomas Jefferson when he resigned the Administration to James Madison on March 4, 1809. He returned to his home in Monticello and lived a quiet life for seventeen years. He remained until his dying day an ardent Democrat.

To illustrate how firmly Mr. Jefferson believed in the "newly found" democracy in America is reflected in his words: "Would the honest patriot, in the full tide of successful experiment, abandon a government which has so far kept us free and firm, on the theoretic and visionary fear that this government, the world's best hope, may by possibility want energy to preserve itself? I trust not. I believe this, on the contrary the strongest government on earth." [23]

"Jefferson's interest and talents covered an amazing range. He became the foremost American architect of his time. He designed the Virginia Capitol, the University of Virginia, and his own home, Monticello. As a scientific farmer, he cultivated the finest gardens in America. His many inventions included the swivel chair and the dumb waiter. Jefferson's excellent library became the nucleus of the Library of Congress. He drafted Virginia's civil code, and founded its state university. He devised the convenient decimal system of coinage that allows Americans to keep accounts in dollars and cents. He prepared written vocabularies of Indian languages." [24]

It was the genius of Jefferson above all men that instilled the spirit of democracy into American life and put the seal of the true republicanism on the nation's institutions. Democracy has won in the United States, and

---

[22] Jefferson," *World Book Encyclopedia, X* (1962). P. 68
[23] Schorer, *op. cit.* P. 126
[24] "Jefferson," *op. cit.* P. 58.

the spirit of its founder lives in all our political parties. He stamped his individuality on the American nation more than any other man. Democracy is supreme in this country. In all matters of government the people rule, except where their own lethargy has suffered the political boss to gain a temporary ascendancy. If combinations of the wealth or other interests gain control of the government it is because the people do not use the machinery that is in their hands. We have also nationality, strong and firm; but this has its being only at the will of the democracy. All constitutions, laws, congresses, and courts are subjects to this great, final national tribunal—the People. No statesman can rise above and disregard this power; no act of Congress is so stable that it may not be ground to power by the ponderous weight of public opinion. This vast being, the Public, has discovered his strength, and it was Thomas Jefferson above all men who awakened him to self-consciousness." [25]

The tall red-haired Virginian believed that "those who labor in the earth are the chosen people of God."

There was much controversy over his religious beliefs. "Many of his contemporaries were of the opinion that he was an atheist, or at least an infidel . . . These beliefs probably had their origin in the part he played in disestablishing the Church in Virginia, and in certain excerpts from his writings. While Jefferson was a vestryman in the Episcopal Church for many years, to the time of his death, he was very broad in his religious views, and made no quarrel with his neighbor for believing in one God or twenty gods. He had no patience with Puritanism, and his strife with the New England clergy ended only with his public life. There is no doubt that he was sincere and even devout. He pronounced Christianity as the purest and sublimest system of morals ever delivered to man. To John Adams he wrote: "An atheist I can never be. I am a Christian in the only sense Christ ever wished one to be." He was doubtless a man of pure morals, notwithstanding the attacks of some of his enemies." [26]

"In his old age, he wrote: "To love God with all thy heart and thy neighbor as thyself is the sum of religion." [27]

---

[25] Elson, *op. cit.* P. 381.
[26] Elson, *op. cit.* P. 379.
[27] *Ibid.* P. 380

"Fifty years to the day after the Declaration of Independence had been adopted, John Adams died in Quincy, Massachusetts. "Jefferson still lives," ex-President Adams murmured on his deathbed. But in Virginia, a few hours earlier on that same day, July 4, 1826—Thomas Jefferson had also died." [28]

His self-written epitaph reads: "Here was buried Thomas Jefferson, author of the Declaration of Independence, the Statute of Virginia for religious freedom, and father of the University of Virginia." Freedom—political, religious, intellectual—had been his lifelong preoccupation. President he had been, and Vice President and Secretary of State and Ambassador, but Jefferson's epitaph, ignoring these honors makes clear the achievements by which he wanted to be remembered." [29]

---

[28] Schorer, *op. cit*. P. 172.

[29] Ibid. P. 172.

Bibliography

1. Bailey, Matilda, and Leavell, Ullin W., *A World of American Literature*, American Book Company, New York, 1963
2. Chinard, Gilbert, Thomas Jefferson: *The Apostle of Americanism*, University of Michigan Press, Ann Arbor, Michigan, 1957.
3. De Vries, Julian, *Lives of the Presidents*, World Publishing Company, Cleveland, Ohio, 1944.
4. Early, James, Frier, Robert, Ellison, Emily, Gurney, A.R. Sick, Jean, Eisenhauer, Louis, and Folds, Thomas M., *Adventures In American Literature*, Harcourt, Brace, and World Inc., New York, 1968.
5. Elson, Henry William, *History of the United States of America*, The Macmillan Company, New York, 1957.
6. Hockett, Homer Carey, *Political and Social Growth of the American People*, 1492-1865, The Macmillan Company, New York, 1940.
7. Miers, Earl Schenck, *The Story of Thomas Jefferson*, Grossett and Dunlap, New York, 1955.
8. Preston, Ralph C., and Tottle, John, *In These United States and Canada*, D.C. Health and Company, Boston, 1965.
9. Schorer, Mark, Jewett, Arno, Havighurst, Walter, and Kirschner, Allen, *American Literature*, Houghton Mifflin Company, Boston, 1968.
10. Sheean, Vincent, Thomas Jefferson: *Father of Democracy*, Random House, New York, 1953.
11. *The World Book Encyclopedia*, Field Enterprises Educational Corporation, Chicago, Illinois, 1962.

Rh Blood Factor and Its Importance

Karl Landsteiner and Alexander Wiener in 1940 discovered the Rh blood factor as an important cause of stillbirths.

The Rh factor is present in the red blood cells of approximately 85 percent of human beings. Serious and often fatal reactions can occur if doctors do not match Rh groups when giving transfusions, or if a mother who does not have the Rh factor gives birth to an infant who does have the Rh factor.

"Rh factor is a substance in the red blood cells of most persons. When this substance combines with a particular member of a group of proteins called agglutinins, it causes the red blood cells to agglutinate, or clump. This reaction may produce serious illness or death. Persons who have the Rh factor are known as Rh positive. Those who do not have the Rh factor are Rh-negative." [1]

The Rh factor is inherited. The child of an Rh-negative mother and an Rh-positive father may be Rh-positive. Before birth, some of the baby's blood cells may enter the mother's blood. Then the mother may build up Rh antibodies. The antibodies may return to the baby's blood. This reaction usually does not cause trouble for the first child. But the number of antibodies in the mother's blood may build up enough to harm a second Rh-positive child. This may result in severe anemia, brain damage, or death.

---

[1] *World Book Encyclopedia*. Vol. 15. P. 271.

A severe reaction takes place in only about one of twenty Rh-negative women married to Rh-positive men. If the mother's blood is tested and observed for antibodies during pregnancy, a doctor can treat trouble if it occurs. Treatment usually involves completely replacing the baby's blood with fresh blood." [2]

Doctors have known for years that people can be divided into groups according to certain factors in the blood which react with factors of a different type in other blood. The blood of some groups may be mixed without danger. In some cases, the fluid matter in the blood of one person will coagulate the red blood cells of another. This is of the greatest importance in blood transfusion. Through previous tests, it is a known fact that "O" blood can be mixed without any danger. The "A" and "B" classifications have been made to indicate when transfusions are safe and when they are not.

In recent years, the Rh factor has been discovered. This factor has another protein substance that causes serious effect if uncontrolled.

In legal cases, the Rh factor has been found to be useful in determining if a certain man can be the father of a certain child.

The disease, "erythroblastosis," occurs when the Rh factor is improperly mixed. This disease breaks up the blood vessels of the baby and may cause death.

There are four known Rh factors; however only the Rh(d) factor has clinical importance.

Landsteiner and Wiener made their test on a Rhesus monkey. As a results of their findings another protein substance in the red corpuscles of this monkey, they named the newly found substance for the monkey.

The Rh factor is of importance to every human being because it could decide who will or who will not live; however in the hands of skilled and trained physicians, the chance of survival is good.

---

[2] *Ibid.*

Bibliography

1. Otto, James H. and Towle, Albert, *Modern Biology*. Holt, Rinehart, and Winston, Inc., New York. 1965. Chapter 11, P. 162/Chapter 42. P. 587.
2. Fishbein, Morris, M.D., *Home Medical Adviser*. Doubleday & Co., Inc., Garden City, N.Y. 1963. P. 280 & P. 371.
3. *World Book Encyclopedia*, Field Enterprises Educational Corporation, Chicago, Ill. 1962. Volumes 2, 11, 15 and 17.

Latin Literature

Man's knowledge of the beginnings of Latin literature is very limited. We have in our possession only a few fragments of pre-literary writings and from these and the remarks made by later writers, it is known that this early literature consisted mainly of hymns, laws, and official records.

The date, 272 B.C., is usually given for the beginning of Latin literature as we know it today; however formal Latin literature began in 240 B.C., when a Roman audience saw a Latin version of a Greek play.

Livius Andronicus, a slave, upon receiving his freedom about 272 B.C., translated Homer's *Odyssey* into an old type of Latin verse known as the Saturnian's measure. He also presented Latin versions of Greek dramas in both tragedy and comedy.

Following Andronicus, the poet, Gnaeus Naevius, wrote an epic on the first Punic War. His dramas were mainly reworkings of Greek originals. He created a form of tragedy purely Roman in content.

Of even more importance than Naevius was Quintus Ennius, a poet, who wrote the historical epic, the *Annals*. This poem, of which we have only a few hundred lines, was written in hexameters instead of the monotonous Saturnian meter.

After Ennius, Roman epic poetry was neglected for a century. Tragedy, on the other hand, flourished, because of the constant demand for new plays to be presented at popular festivals.

In the field of tragic dramas, Marcus Pacuvius and Lucius Accius followed after Ennius. Only fragments of their plays survive.

The Latin literature that we possess is richer in comedy than in tragedy. We have 20 complete comedy plays by Plautus and the entire work, six plays by Terence. These men modeled their plays on Greek comedies. Plautus used many songs in his plays. These songs, although the music has been lost, show that the Italians loved singing—then and now.

Cato, (234-149 B.C.), wrote the first Latin history of Rome. He also wrote speeches and a manual on farming, *De agri cultura*.

Gaius Lucilius (180-102 B.C.), a fluent and prolific writer, created a new kind of literature in his thirty books of *Satires*. He indulged in the practice of singling out individuals for personal attack in many of his satires.

"Latin literature reached its period of greatest art from 106 B.C. to A.D. 14—that is, from the birth of Cicero to the death of the emperor Augustus." [1]

The four decades that elapsed between the dictatorship of Sulla and the death of Cicero (106-42 B.C.) comprise one of the two great periods in the history of Latin literature. Latin prose, during this period, was raised to its highest level by Cicero. He wrote letters, rhetorical treatises, philosophical works, and orations. No figure ranks higher in the history of Latin literature than Cicero.

During the reign of the emperor, Augustus, Latin literature flourished. The principal poet of this period, Virgil, is also the greatest poet in all Latin literature. Some of his works are his *Eclogues*, Georgics, and Aeneid. Virgil's contemporary, Horace, wrote Epodes, Odes, Satires, and Epistles.

"The Latin elegy reached its highest development in the works of Tibullus (48-19 B.C.), Propertius (50-16 B.C.), and Ovid (43 B.C.-17A.D.). Most of this poetry is concerned with love. But we remember Ovid most for his Metamorphoses, which served as a reference work on mythology for hundreds of years." [2]

---

[1] *World Book Encyclopedia.* Vol. 11. P.105
[2] *Ibid.*

Latin prose did not reach the same level as did Augustan poetry. Livy and Seneca were the chief prose writers of this era. Livy produced a history of the Roman people in 142 books. The thirty-five which survive are a major source of information on Rome. Seneca wrote nine tragedies and several ethical works.

Lucan wrote the Pharsalia, and epic poem, describing the civil war between Caesar and Pompey.

Petronicus wrote Satyr icon, the first realistic novel in Western literature.

Tacitus in his *Histories* and *Annals*, was one of the best prose writers of his time.

Pliny, Quintilian, Aulus Gellius, Fronto, Lucius Apuleius, and Seutonius placed their names in the prose writings of Latin literature.

Quintilian composed the most complete work on ancient education. Gellius wrote a series of essays depicting Roman life and literature. The letters of Pliny vividly described Roman life of his period. Suetonius wrote biographies of the 12 Roman rulers from Julius Caesar through Domitian. Apuleius wrote *The Golden Ass*, a fascinating story of adventure.

Bibliography

1. *The World Book Encyclopedia*, Volume 11, Field Enterprises Educational Corporation, Chicago, Ill.
2. *Italy*, Kish, George, Nelson Doubleday, Inc., Garden City, N.Y.
3. *The Best of The World's Classics*, Vole II, Rome, by Lodge, Henry Cabot and Halsey, Francis, Funk & Wagnall's Co., N.Y.
4. *Lays of Ancient Rome and Other Poems*, Macaulay, Thomas, Worthington Company, New York.

Chapter 10

(A Christian Drama; Matt. 24:42-46)
My Mama; The Writer, Editor, and Director

"The Travelers Guide to Heaven"

"The Travelers Guide to Heaven"

Congregational Song: "Jesus Is Getting Us Ready for That Great Day."

Soloist: "Coming Home." *<At Rear of auditorium>*

Narrator: This world is not our home. We are Pilgrim travelers on our way to our final destination. Jesus said to a man of the Pharisees, a ruler of the Jews who came to Him by night, "Except a man be born of the water, and of the Spirit he cannot enter into the kingdom of God. Marvel not that I say unto thee, "Ye must be born again." It is when we are born again that we receive our reservations for thereby we meet the challenge of preparation which includes regeneration, perfected by constant re-dedication.

Blessed are the born again souls who are heaven bound at last. I say to you the city which God has prepared is as imperishable in its inhabitants as its material. The city with twelve gates of Pearl, jasper, silver and gold . . . Praise God the day has come and another host has come to join the 144,000. We are traveling on board for Canaan Land.

Soloist: "Come And Go With Me To That Land" or "I am Bound for Canaan Land."

1st Traveler: Is this where you get your ticket?

Narrator: Yes, your name please!

1st Traveler: Oh, it is not in the book; that's why I am here to pick it up. I want to register before the crowd gets here.

Narrator: Sorry! Tickets only by reservation. You earn your ticket by working in the Vineyard. Heaven must be in you before you can be in heaven. You can't buy a ticket for this heavenly flight. Your ticket is a written pledge signed and guaranteed . . . the blood makes this possible. It can only be claimed and its promise kept by working out your own salvation. <*1st Traveler walks away.*>

2nd Traveler: <*Rushes up to the window*>
 Praise God I am ready, all except my vaccination and inoculation.

Narrator: My dear Sister, injections are not needed, as diseases are unknown in Heaven. Just relax, Jesus has made ready a perfect kingdom of love, joy, peace, and we shall all possess a changed body.

3rd Traveler: Good evening . . . Praise God from whom all blessings flow. I am here to pick up my reservations.

Narrator: Grace be unto you, Sister. Your reservation is written in the Lamb's Book of Life. <*3rd Traveler goes inside Plane*>.

4th Traveler: <*Walks Up to Window*>

Narrator: May I have your confirmation!

4th Traveler: It has been a long journey. If you wonder how I got over it was grace and only grace. I see the sign says, Reservation only. Praise God, I made my reservations 25 years ago at Jackson, Mississippi Chapel Hill Baptist International Airport to join the Pilgrim travelers.

 At first I was not sure. I could not find peace. Then, I said, "Lord I am going to pray this prayer and I am not going to pray any more." Right then and there the 3rd member of the Holy Trinity confirmed my reservations, started me out on preparation, and now I am so determined to reach my final destination. The Lord is my light and my salvation, whom then shall I fear. I shall not be afraid because I know a great Savior. Don't you?

5th Traveler: <*Cripple man comes down aisle as soft music is played.*>

5th Traveler: "I am coming Lord; for 60 years I have been trusting in your Word. In my Father's house are many mansions; if it were not so I would have told you. You went and got my place prepared. Thank you Lord. I am on my way. My reservations are right here." <*Hands up; rejoicing.*>

Soloist: "I'll Go"

<*Cripple man leans over on his crutches until the song is finished, then continues walking toward the plane*>

Cripple Man: Well, I am nearer than I was yesterday. Some day I will be where the great mansions are, near the great white throne near the great jasper sea, near the bound of life where I can lay my burden down, nearer bearing my cross, nearer my wearing the crown!

Narrator: Your name is on record Soldier, take your reservation over there.

6th Traveler: <*A well-dressed man walks up to the ticket office. He takes out a large roll of money. Holding up his picture.*>

Well Madam, here is my picture and here are my papers with the proper credentials.

Narrator: Sir, I am sorry, we do not need your picture. The Father knows the face of every child. Your credentials are worthless. Revelations 21:27 tells us, "There shall in no wise enter into it anything that shall defileth, neither whatsoever worketh abomination, or he that maketh a lie: but they which are written in the Lamb's book of life."

<*Narrator gives man (6th Traveler), everything back*>.
<*Man walks away—head down.*>

7th Traveler: <*A woman comes with her suitcase*>
I only have one piece of baggage to take through customs.

Narrator: No luggage whatsoever can be taken. We brought nothing into this world and it is certain we can carry nothing out, only one declaration is required while going through customs. I Corinthians 15:1-2 says; "Moreover brethren, I declare unto you the Gospel which I preached unto you, which also ye have received, and wherein ye stand. By which also ye are saved if ye keep in memory what I preached unto you, unless ye have believed in vain."

7th Traveler: <Drops suitcase>
"O God forgive me I do remember all Thy Precious Words. Passengers are classified as immigrants since we are taking up permanent residence . . . A new country that is heavenly wherefore God is not ashamed to be called our God for He hath prepared for us a city."

8th Traveler: <Woman walks slowly>

Narrator: Sister, May I serve you today?

8th Traveler: No, Dear Recorder—my reservation is not for today. The fields are white, the harvest waiting, the laborers so few. I just came to get someone to take a message to the other side. I want my mother, father, sisters, brothers and friends to know that when my work is done, to look for me. I am coming home some day. <Sits down, smiling . . . . >

Soloist: "There Will be Peace In The Valley Some Day"

9th Traveler: Romans 1:16 says and is my testimony . . . "I am not ashamed of the Gospel of Jesus Christ for it is the power of God unto salvation to everyone that believeth, to the Jew first, and also to the Greek." I purchased my ticket at Louisiana's Pearly Grove Baptist Airport on the 1920th year of our Lord and Savior Christ. I was given instructions by an old Baptist Preacher who could hardly read this map <Holds up Bible> of directions, but this old fashioned announcement clerk knew the Pilot, the one and only Christ, the King of Kings. The Gospel hook he used caught hold of me and fixed me for the journey.

10th Traveler: When I first made an acknowledgment of Christ as my Savior I was not quite ready; my belief was shallow, so I made my way to Gate 'G' the Security Check found Carnal mindedness in my overnight case;

therefore I could not pass the security check because, Romans 8:7 says, "The carnal mind is against God. I decided I would not be out done. I traveled the hypocritical path . . . until one day trouble knocked on my door and just would not stay away. I then prayed to God in earnest, not caring what folk said, I was hungry for the blessing. My poor Soul it would be fed . . . When at last by faith, I touched Him. Like sparks from smiteth steel, just so quickly salvation reached me. O Bless God, I know its real and since that day I have been rising and falling, climbing high mountains, but thanks be to God, I'll make it.

Soloist: "How Great Thou Art"

11th Traveler: I called Reservations and Ticket Information desk 45 years ago. I was informed that the cost was high. I was also informed that the price had been paid out on a hill call Golgotha, but it was mine to fully surrender. I was informed that there was no short cuts, such as night flights, seven to 45 days flight, and no such thing as a "No thrills" flight.

I kept on calling one Thursday night, as I heard the co-pilot saying from Isaiah 35:8 "And a highway shall be there, and a way, and it shall be called the way of holiness; unclean shall not pass over it, but it shall be for those—the wayfaring men though fools shall not err therein, no lion shall be there, nor any ravenous beast shall go up thereon, it shall not be found there, but, the redeemed shall walk there . . . a burning sensation ran through my heart all around my heart, tears filled my eyes, my tongue started talking, my feet started walking, I said I wasn't going to tell anybody, but I just couldn't keep it to myself.

Soloist: "I Couldn't Keep It To My self"

12th Traveler: I was on a stand by flight at the Texas Morning Star Baptist Airport, sitting there on the mourner's bench. I was seeking for eternal reservations to place my poor anxious soul on flight 1935. I was kept on stand-by because I wanted to see something, I wanted to hear something. In fact, I wanted a sign. Finally, the co-pilot said, "If thou shalt confess with thy mouth the Lord Jesus, and shalt believe in thine heart that God hath raised Him from the dead, thou shalt be saved. (Romans 10:9) Now I can't help what this new generation says, I heard . . . I mean I heard the singing in the trees, I heard the voice of Jesus say," Come unto me and rest. Lay down thy weary one lay down, thy head upon my breast. There I sat on stand-by until finally I couldn't sit any longer . . . so I came to Jesus just as I was weary; wound, and sad. I found in Him a resting place and He has made me glad.

Song: "I Heard The Voice Of Jesus Say"

Stewardess: Good Morning . . . . And now your Captain speaks.

Pilot: This is your Pilot Captain—speaking . . . I have overcome the world!

Jesus: Flight 1979 *(current year)*, is now airborne . . . God shall wipe all tears from our eyes.

~Closing Scene~

ALL: "Come on, Come on, don't you want to go?"

~*The End*~

13th Traveler: I have been waiting a long time to take my flight on the Holy Ghost Air Lines. Tell me when will I get aboard?

Narrator: My dear Sister, the date of your departure has not been announced. Travelers are advised to be prepared to leave at short notice. It is not for you to know the time or season, only God the Father knows that.

13th Traveler: Thank you, my sister.

Solo: "When He Calls Me—I Will Answer."

14th Traveler: I am here to tell my friends and kindred that are about to take their flight to that beautiful city beyond the sky, that each day, I am listening for my name. *<Turns to audience>*

My Lord what a morning its going to be! Praise God, I have my crown in lay away. Thank you Jesus, I will meet you at the coronation . . . Thank You! Thank You! Thank You Jesus! *<Joins Group>*

Chapter 11

My Mama's Biography

Biography of My Mama: Mrs. Louisteen {Wilkerson} Bolding-Harris

    The Booker T. Washington PTA honored Mrs. Louisteen Bolding Harris, fourth grade teacher at the school with a reception on Sunday afternoon, May 15, 1983. The occasion was Mrs. Harris' retirement after 32 years of teaching. All former students and friends were invited to the reception and urged to attend.

    Mrs. Harris was born in Hugo, Oklahoma and received her basic education in the Hugo Public Schools. She married Leveorn Harris, who retired from the Oklahoma State University, County of Choctaw Extension 4-H agent. After retirement, was an elected City Councilman official of the City of Hugo, Oklahoma. The Harris' have two children, eldest, Patricia L. Harris-Cook of Oklahoma City, Oklahoma and Tony Leveorn Harris of Houston Texas. They also have four grandsons; Raymond L. Cook Jr., Reginald L. Cook, Jacob and Joshua Harris, twins born August 2000.

    Mrs. Louisteen Bolding Harris' first two years in the teaching profession were spent at the Lake View School in the Frogville, Oklahoma community. Mrs. Harris taught the first and second grades, and coached the seventh and eighth grade basketball girl's teams.

    The next two years Mrs. Harris taught third and fourth grades at the Bluff Elementary School, a rural community, south of Hugo, Oklahoma. The last 28 years were spent in the Hugo City Public Schools, at Booker T. Washington and Robert E. Lee Elementary Schools.

    Mrs. Harris was valedictorian of her Junior High School class.

She was salutatorian at Booker T. Washington High School; Cum laude at Langston University; recipient of a Human Relations grant at Oklahoma University; Head Start Certificates of Service in 1965, 1968 and 1970; Outstanding Elementary Teacher of America Award, 1972; Teacher of the Year, Robert E. Lee Elementary School, Hugo, OK, 1978.

Mrs. Harris received her B.A. degree from Langston University and her Masters from Southeastern Oklahoma State University.

During the summer of 1968, Mrs. Harris served as a social worker for Choctaw County Head Start Programs. In 1970 she was selected as director of Head Start Program of Hugo.

Mrs. Harris is a member of Hugo Chapel Baptist Church, Belles Lettres Club, Iota Beta Chi Sorority, OEA, NEA, and ACT. Indeed she touched the lives of many families.

All in all, a remarkable woman. The teaching profession will sorely miss her.

Patricia L. Harris-Cook, Daughter

Mrs. Louisteen Harris passes
(Newspaper article)

Again death has invaded the ranks of the Hugo Chapel Missionary Baptist Church and carried away a faithful member; A Godly life ended on September 19, 1993

Mrs. Louisteen Bolding-Harris was born April 17, 1927 in Hugo, Oklahoma, Gay Community to Louie and Lucille (Wilkerson) Bolding, into a family of six, four sisters; Rosie, Mary, Lucy-Doris, and two brothers; Rafie, and Amos Bolding.

She united in marriage to Mr. Leveorn Harris from Broken Bow, Oklahoma. They were wed in Hugo, Oklahoma. The beauty of her life will always be remembered.

At an early age she became a Christian and began her work for Christ, uniting with Hugo Chapel Missionary Baptist Church as a young adult. Here Mrs. Harris remained a faithful member serving as Church Clerk, Junior Sunday School Class Teacher, Usher, Nurse, President and Mission Bible Instructor, never refusing a task, a challenge, and never too tired. Her loyalty to the Church, South Central Oklahoma District and its work was witnessed by many until ill health and finally death.

My Mama, Louisteen Bolding-Harris,
Would Do It Again! *Newspaper article 1983*

Editor's Note: They are unsung heroes. They may have more influence on our society than any other single element and yet they receive little recognition. They're the lifetime teachers, those who, in spite of low pay and little appreciation, give their lives to providing others the tools they will need to survive in today's world. The following story is one of a series on such teachers in the Hugo, Oklahoma and Paris, Texas area. Each of the teachers included in the series retired at the close of the 1983 school year.

The Paris News, Monday, July 11, 1983;
Retiring Teacher—Louisteen Harris, a Hugo elementary teacher recently retired with 32 years of service, received a silver platter given to her by the faculty upon her retirement. "I would really go back and do it all again. It (teaching) is a rewarding experience in spite of the changes . . . When you can see that a kid has done well, it makes you feel good." Those were the words of Mrs. Louisteen Harris in a recent interview with the Paris News in which she looked back over her career as a teacher.

Mrs. Harris, an elementary teacher in the Hugo Independent School District, retired at the close of the 1983 school year, ending a 32-year career.

Mrs. Harris began her career in 1947 teaching first and second grades in Lakeview, Oklahoma, 25 miles east of Hugo. Two years later she taught third and fourth grades in Bluff, Oklahoma, a small community approximately 20 miles southwest of Hugo, Oklahoma. In 1955 she began her tenure as a fourth grade teacher in Hugo public schools and has been within the district until her retirement this year (1983).

Mrs. Harris said she has seen many changes during her teaching career. Among them she mentioned discipline. "Almost anything was okay when I first started teaching. Now, I'm almost half afraid to discipline a child if I don't know the parents."

"I was never much for beating a kid—it had no effect if they got it at home all the time," she said." "This year we all tried assertive discipline and it has worked well," she said, explaining that a letter was sent home with each child to parents, outline exactly what steps would be taken in the discipline process,"

"Mrs. Harris explained, "The parents had to sign the letters and state on them if they prohibited any of the measures. It worked because the kids knew what the punishment would be, but they also knew the rewards for being good too," she added.

Some of the rewards, she said, were an extra 10 minutes of playtime on Fridays, an extra trip to the library, or collecting points to receive a good behavior certificate from the principal.

Another change Mrs. Harris said she has noted is the change in curriculum. "They added too much. Kids will be exposed to some of those things without having a specific class on them. They stress the non-basics, but the trend in back to the basics now," she said.

"I was glad when they changed from the new math. It confused so many people,'" she added.

Mrs. Harris expressed enthusiasm over one of the more recent changes, the addition of computers in the classroom. There is one per classroom, and students rotate using it. There are tapes on every subject, she said, and tapes could be made to fit to a student's specific problem. "The kids love them—they never get tired of working on the computer," she added.

The retired teacher also commented on a change in student attitudes over the years. "They don't think it (education) is as important as kids did in previous years. It takes so much more to motivate them nowadays."

She also said most of today's children are involved in some kind of extra-curricula activity nearly every night. "We want the children to be involved, but not to the point that schoolwork suffers."

Mrs. Harris sees education in the future on the upward swing; "if they keep getting back to the basics. Assertive discipline will help, too. It's one of the best things to happen (to education)," she said.

One of Mrs. Harris' favorite memories, she said, is having been a seventh and eighth grade girl's basketball coach. "It was my first year to teach, and the principal said I would be a good coach. I told him I didn't know a thing about basketball, but he said I could order a book," she remembers. When the book didn't get there by the beginning of the season, the "coach," (Mrs. Harris), had to tell the players she did not know how to coach. "That's okay, 'they said,' we know how to play—we just need someone to supervise us.'" Mrs. Harris recalled. "They had previously had a good coach before me. Then I got interested and learned to play myself. I got pretty good, too."

Mrs. Harris, the former Louisteen Bolding, is a Hugo, Oklahoma native. She married Leveorn Harris in 1949. Their daughter, Patricia L. Harris-Cook resides in Oklahoma City, Oklahoma, and their son, Tony Leveorn Harris, lives in Los Angeles, California *(currently, Houston, Texas)*. Tony was a teacher and coach in the Texas community of Orange for four years, prior to moving to L.A. Mrs. Harris has two grandchildren, Raymond L. Cook, Jr. and Reginald L. Cook. *(Year to date; two additions, twin grandson's, Joshua and Jacob Harris, born in 2000.)*

Mrs. Harris received her bachelor's degree in 1951 in elementary education from Langston University in Langston, Oklahoma. She earned her master's degree in 1958 from Southeastern State College in Durant, Oklahoma.

Now that she is retired, Mrs. Harris said she plans to do some traveling to visit relatives, do volunteer work at the hospital, work with youth groups at her church and enjoy being a housewife. "I like to cook, sew and all those kind of things," she said.

An active member of the Hugo Chapel Baptist Church, Belles Lettres service organization, and various teaching organizations such as National Education Association (NEA), and Oklahoma Education Association (OEA). Mrs. Harris said that she also plans to join the Retired Teachers Association (RTA).

Mrs. Harris was given a reception upon her retirement and was presented with an engraved silver tray and a bracelet from the faculty. Her walls are also adorned with numerous plagues of appreciation from the Belles Lettres and her church.

"Teaching was not what I had visualized, but once I started, it grew on me, I didn't really want to do anything else," Mrs. Harris said.

Article by: Carla Rheudasil News Staff Writer

Patricia L. Harris-Cook, Daughter

A Few of My Mama's Favorite Recipes

Pecan Pie (small pie)
1 C. Sugar
1 C. (Karo) Syrup
1/2 C. butter (1 stick)
3 eggs (beat one at a time)
1 t. Vanilla
1/8 t. Salt
1/4 t. nutmeg
1/4 t. cinnamon
1 C. Pecans

Mix ingredients well. Put in Pie crust. Bake at 350 for 40 minutes.

* * *

Tea Cakes
1/2 C. Butter or Margarine
1 C. Sugar
2 eggs, beaten
1 t. Vanilla
3 1/2 cups sifted flour
1 t. baking power
1/2 t. salt
1/2 t. nutmeg
1/2 C. dairy sour cream

Cream butter/sugar until light and fluffy.
Blend in eggs/vanilla.
Add combined dry ingredients alternately with sour cream, mixing well after each addition.
Chill several hours or overnight.
On lightly floured surface, roll out dough to 1/4 inch thickness; cut dough with 3-in round cookie cutter.
Place on well greased cookie skeet; sprinkle with sugar.
Bake at 450 degrees for 12 minutes, or until lightly browned.
Yields: Approximate two dozens. (Try them, and enjoy!)

* * *

My Mama's Best Pound Cake
1 C. butter
1 2/3 C. sugar
5 eggs
2 C. Cake flour
1/4 t. salt
1 t. vanilla
1 t. lemon juice

Grated rind of 1/2 lemon

Preheat oven 350 degrees.
Cream butter—add sugar . . .
—beat until light and fluffy, as whipped cream.
Add eggs—one at a time—beat hard after each addition.
Do not add another egg—until batter is smooth and fluffy each time.
Sift flour and measure . . . then sift again with salt.
Fold dry ingredients into creamed mixture in about four portions, mix until batter is smooth and has absorbed ingredients.
Do not over beat.
Add vanilla, lemon juice and lemon rind.
Line bottom of oiled 5 1/2 by 9 inch loaf pan or tube pan with brown paper.
Oil the paper and fill with mixture. Bake for 50 minutes

Patricia L. Harris-Cook, Daughter

This is a copy of a reading in Mama's journal in her original hand-writing: "Why We Celebrate Children's Day." By Louisteen Bolding-Harris

Why We Celebrate Children's Day

The observance of the second Sunday in June as Children's Day by the Protestant churches began in the middle of the last century. It fell on June 10, 1945. The earliest recorded observance was arranged by the Rev. Dr. Charles H. Leonard, pastor of the Universalist Church of the Redeemer in Chelsea, Mass., the second Sunday in June 1856. A special service was held for the children and those who had not been baptized were christened. Dr. Leonard called the day Rose Sunday. The day was later called Flower Sunday, but in the course of a few years it came to be known as Children's Day.

The Methodist Episcopal Church was the first denomination formally to recognize the day. Its adoption was recommended in 1866, and in 1868 the general conference voted the second Sunday in June be observed in honor of the children.

Like many American customs the observance of Children's Day has its roots in the old world. May Day was the day on which children were confirmed in the Roman and the Lutheran churches. The children carried flowers in a procession to the churches. This is probably why Children's Day was first called Rose Day or Flower Day. The change from May Day to June is a natural shifting of the date to conform to the season of flowers, especially in the southern part of the country.

Mrs. Louisteen Bolding Harris; Outstanding Elementary Teachers of America (1972 Edition)

This honor is given to men and women whose devotion has not only encompassed the social and intellectual development of the children and teenagers who are their students but, has led them to give outstanding service to their communities, as well as their profession.

Every year in late summer and early fall, millions of school-age children take their places in classrooms across the nation. Whether these rooms are located in large, modern educational facilities or among the few remaining one-room school houses is of less importance than the quality of the teachers. For the next nine or ten months, these individuals will make profound impression on the students entrusted to them. They will instruct their students, and they will help shape budding attitudes toward education and other aspects of society which will prevail for the rest of their lives.

The more than 9,000 men and women who accomplishments appear on the following pages reflect in their contributions to their professional fields and their communities' appreciation of the extraordinary responsibilities which they have assumed. Through published works, they share experiences and finding which serve to broaden educational knowledge. Through civic endeavors, they provide a means for interchanging ideas between school systems and communities—enriching both in the process.

Educators selected for citation here have received a distinct honor. They were nominated for national recognition by their superintendents of education or by their principals. The Board of Editors of Outstanding Elementary Teachers of America, which includes leader of secondary education, believes these selection truly reflect standards of excellence.

The board salutes the dedicated men and women included in this volume. Their achievements highlight the bright future of American Education and the promise awaiting millions of young people who will soon be part of that system.

Harris-Louisteen Bolding

"Hugo, Oklahoma: Born: April 17, 1927; Married: Leveorn; Children: Patricia Lucille, Tony Leveorn; Parents: Louie and Lucille Bolding; Roosevelt and Osie Harris.

Education: Langston University, Bachelor of Arts (BA) cum laude 1945-51; Southeastern State College, Master's Degree, MAT 1956-58; Career: Teacher; Robert E. Lee School 1968-1972 (*Special Note, Retired Robert E. Lee Elementary, 1983*), Booker T. Washington School 1955-68, Bluff Public School 1950-1951; Washington Elementary School, Head Start Director 1970; Choctaw County Head Start, Social Worker 1968; Lakeview Public School Teacher, Principal, Basketball Coach 1947-50; Civic: National Education Association (NEA); Oklahoma Education Association (OEA); Choctaw County Teacher Association, Program Committee; Belles Lettres Club, Secretary; Langston Alumni Association, Secretary; Robert E. Lee Parent Teacher Association (PTA), Secretary; Chamber of Commerce, Hospital Committee; Baptist Church, Sunday School, Baptist Training Union (BTU) Director, Missionary Program Chairperson, Usher Board Chairperson/Director/Secretary; South Central (Oklahoma) District Association, Recreation Leader; Iota Beta Chi, Reporter; Honors: High School Salutatorian 1944; Human Relations Grant, Oklahoma University 1963; Head Start Certification 1965, 1968" [1]

---

[1] *Outstanding Elementary Teachers of America* MCMLXXII, 1120 Connecticut Ave., N.W. Washington, D.C.

Get Published, Inc!
Thorofare, NJ 08086
09 September 2009
BA2009252